# TAPPING THE ICEBERG

Achieve Straight A's in life through
**Attitude**, **Aptitude**, and **Action**

# TIM CORK

BASTIAN
BOOKS

Bastian Books
A division of Bastian Publishing Services Ltd.
Toronto, Canada
www.bastianpubserv.com

Distributed by Publishers Group Canada
www.pgcbooks.ca

ISBN 0-9780554-5-4

Cataloguing in Publication Data available from Library and Archives Canada.

*Editorial:* Donald G. Bastian, Bastian Publishing Services Ltd.,
www.bastianpubserv.com

*Book design:* Olena Sullivan, New Mediatrix, www.olena.ca

Printed in Canada by Webcom

In the spirit of giving, a portion of the proceeds from sales of this book will be donated to the Taylor Statten Camping Bursary Fund, which helps less fortunate kids go to summer camp.

# ABOUT THE AUTHOR

 Tim Cork's career spans 20 years in the high-tech, commercial real estate, and communications industries. He has held senior positions, both nationally and internationally, with such companies as Xerox, Regus, and TCS Telecom. He has extensive expertise in major sales initiatives, strategic alliances, people, and change.

Tim is currently the president of NEXCareer, an international provider of Career Transition, Outplacement, and Coaching services. He is much sought after as a speaker and has been published in numerous magazines and newspapers. The *Globe and Mail* has called him "the Networking Guru" and the *Toronto Sun*, "the Career Guru."

Prior to joining NEXCareer, Tim worked as a high-performance coach through his own company, Insight Marketing, where he trained and coached executives and their teams.

Tim lives in Toronto with his wife and two children. He uses his name as an acronym for his purpose in life, which is to Touch, Inspire, and Move people.

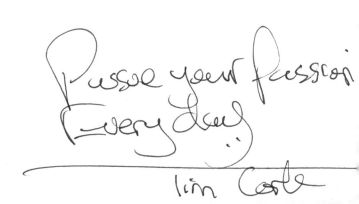

*To my mom, Joan,*
*my hero and the biggest giver I know.*

*And to Suzy, Geoff, and Stephanie:*
*you touch, inspire, and move me every day!*

# CONTENTS

Acknowledgments  ix

Introduction  1

## PART ONE/**ATTITUDE**

Choose Your Attitude. . . . . . . . . . . . . . . . . . . . . . . . . . . . . . 7
Believe in Yourself . . . . . . . . . . . . . . . . . . . . . . . . . . . . . . . 10
Look in the Mirror. . . . . . . . . . . . . . . . . . . . . . . . . . . . . . . 13
That First Impression. . . . . . . . . . . . . . . . . . . . . . . . . . . . . 15
Dream Big, Really Big . . . . . . . . . . . . . . . . . . . . . . . . . . . . 19
Just Imagine ... . . . . . . . . . . . . . . . . . . . . . . . . . . . . . . . . 21
Vision ... the Power of Sight . . . . . . . . . . . . . . . . . . . . . . . 24
Fuel Your Dreams with Passion . . . . . . . . . . . . . . . . . . . . . 26
Ignite the Energy Within . . . . . . . . . . . . . . . . . . . . . . . . . . 28
Release Your Inner Child . . . . . . . . . . . . . . . . . . . . . . . . . . 30
Be Enthusiastic. . . . . . . . . . . . . . . . . . . . . . . . . . . . . . . . . 34
Love Changes Everything. . . . . . . . . . . . . . . . . . . . . . . . . . 36
Forgive and Accept. . . . . . . . . . . . . . . . . . . . . . . . . . . . . . 40
Be the Host . . . . . . . . . . . . . . . . . . . . . . . . . . . . . . . . . . . 43
Be Politely Persistent . . . . . . . . . . . . . . . . . . . . . . . . . . . . 45
Be Confident, Not Arrogant . . . . . . . . . . . . . . . . . . . . . . . 46
How Rude!. . . . . . . . . . . . . . . . . . . . . . . . . . . . . . . . . . . . 48
Integrity ... It's All or Nothing . . . . . . . . . . . . . . . . . . . . . 49
Get Right Back Up . . . . . . . . . . . . . . . . . . . . . . . . . . . . . . 51
Fear ... Friend or Foe? . . . . . . . . . . . . . . . . . . . . . . . . . . . 53
Choose Your Behavior . . . . . . . . . . . . . . . . . . . . . . . . . . . 56
Winners vs. Losers . . . . . . . . . . . . . . . . . . . . . . . . . . . . . . 58
Purpose ... the Big "Why" . . . . . . . . . . . . . . . . . . . . . . . . 60
Uncork Your Possibilities . . . . . . . . . . . . . . . . . . . . . . . . . 61

## PART TWO/**APTITUDE**

What We Learn in Kindergarten . . . . . . . . . . . . . . . . . . . . 65
Knowledge Is Power. . . . . . . . . . . . . . . . . . . . . . . . . . . . . 68
Burden of Proof. . . . . . . . . . . . . . . . . . . . . . . . . . . . . . . . 70
Read the Books . . . . . . . . . . . . . . . . . . . . . . . . . . . . . . . . 73

Juice Your Senses . . . . . . . . . . . . . . . . . . . . . . . . . . . . . . . . 75

Put It in Writing . . . . . . . . . . . . . . . . . . . . . . . . . . . . . . . . 77

It Takes a Team . . . . . . . . . . . . . . . . . . . . . . . . . . . . . . . . . 79

My Three Wise Men . . . . . . . . . . . . . . . . . . . . . . . . . . . . . 82

Be the Teacher . . . . . . . . . . . . . . . . . . . . . . . . . . . . . . . . . . 84

Manage Those Perceptions. . . . . . . . . . . . . . . . . . . . . . . . 86

Think Outside the Box . . . . . . . . . . . . . . . . . . . . . . . . . . 88

The Gift of the Present . . . . . . . . . . . . . . . . . . . . . . . . . . 90

## PART THREE/**ACTION**

Your Success Story . . . . . . . . . . . . . . . . . . . . . . . . . . . . . . 95

Failure (a.k.a. Experience). . . . . . . . . . . . . . . . . . . . . . . 100

Failure = Success. . . . . . . . . . . . . . . . . . . . . . . . . . . . . . . 102

Your Recipe for Success . . . . . . . . . . . . . . . . . . . . . . . . 104

Masterminds of Success . . . . . . . . . . . . . . . . . . . . . . . . 106

Never Stop Moving . . . . . . . . . . . . . . . . . . . . . . . . . . . . 108

Never Stop Networking . . . . . . . . . . . . . . . . . . . . . . . . 109

Join the G7 Club . . . . . . . . . . . . . . . . . . . . . . . . . . . . . . 112

The Elevator Speech. . . . . . . . . . . . . . . . . . . . . . . . . . . . 116

The Art of Cold Calling. . . . . . . . . . . . . . . . . . . . . . . . 118

Set the Right Goals . . . . . . . . . . . . . . . . . . . . . . . . . . . . 122

Create a Goal Action Plan . . . . . . . . . . . . . . . . . . . . . . 125

Achieve Your Goals. . . . . . . . . . . . . . . . . . . . . . . . . . . . 129

Practice the Fundamentals . . . . . . . . . . . . . . . . . . . . . . 132

Keep on Swinging . . . . . . . . . . . . . . . . . . . . . . . . . . . . . 134

Keep a Scorecard . . . . . . . . . . . . . . . . . . . . . . . . . . . . . . 136

Take the Risk . . . . . . . . . . . . . . . . . . . . . . . . . . . . . . . . . 138

Make a Difference . . . . . . . . . . . . . . . . . . . . . . . . . . . . . 139

## PART FOUR/**GETTING STRAIGHT A'S**

The Ten Steps to Getting Straight A's. . . . . . . . . . . . . . 143

Report Card Time!. . . . . . . . . . . . . . . . . . . . . . . . . . . . . 147

Cherish the Moments. . . . . . . . . . . . . . . . . . . . . . . . . . . 149

# ACKNOWLEDGMENTS

*Thank you,*

Allison Quennell, for the many hours you spent helping me with the editing and structure of this book.

Don Bastian, for your tireless support, editing, and ideas; it's great to have an expert on the team.

Stephanie, for helping organize all my journals into the Three A's and then typing from my sticky notes.

Geoff, for your great ideas and quotes – they are always an inspiration.

Suzy, for being my sounding board and inspiration, and for being the Straight-A's person you are.

Olena Sullivan, for making the book look and feel the way I envisioned it – you are a true artist.

Phil Marinucci, for your assistance with conceptual and marketing designs, both in the development of this book and of my website, www.timcork.com.

George Zachanowich, for your genuine enthusiasm, honest feedback, and excellent ideas … and for being a great father-in-law!

*And thank you,*

Jean Hurteau, Ann Firstbrook, Michael Brown, Tom White, Danish Ahmed, Jon Levy, Jim Hayhurst, Jamie Knight, Gord Gibson, Al Zelnick, Dijana Cosic, Deb McKenzie, and Wendy Smith – your support and positive attitude helped me feel good about this project and stay on course.

# INTRODUCTION

*"Whether you believe you can do a thing or not, you are right."*
– Henry Ford

Most people tap very little of their natural potential, leaving many strengths under-developed and under-utilized and many opportunities unrealized. If you're like most people, your greatest talents will remain below the surface, like an iceberg with 90% of its mass under water. Yet this is what must be tapped if you are to realize all the possibilities of your own life.

The question is, how are you going to tap all that strength and potential to achieve your success? I believe the answer is through the Straight A's of Attitude, Aptitude, and Action. It is not a matter of understanding or perfecting any one of the Three A's; it is about practicing and excelling in all three of them in your everyday life. When you have all Three A's in sync, you will have mastered the formula for success. This book is your guide and coach, providing you with a timeless blueprint for learning and living the Straight-A's approach to life.

## Attitude

Your **Attitude** is the first thing people notice about you when you walk into a room. You have fewer than ten seconds to create a positive first impression. Your attitude determines how you are perceived and how successful you will be in accomplishing your goals. If you feel good about yourself, so will the people you meet – as long as your confidence is genuine. Likeability is instantaneous. If there is no chemistry, then there is no connection, no relationship, no job, no potential … and on and on the no's will roll.

> **Attitude is a big thing that makes a big difference.**

Attitude operates by the law of attraction. If you are in a room with some-one who is arrogant, you want to get out of there. If you're in a room with some-one who exudes confidence and charisma, you want to stay and catch the per-son's positive vibes.

You choose your attitude and that attitude will make or break every interaction you ever have. It will determine the outcome.

Above the surface, attitude is expressed in body language and self-esteem. Below the surface, it is made up of your values, dreams, desires, beliefs, and passions. Through tapping what's below the surface, you develop, shape, and release amazing power – for yourself and others.

## Aptitude

After their initial, instantaneous assessment of you, people will continue to judge you on your **Aptitude**. They will want to know your background or experiences and evaluate your ability to answer questions and handle certain circumstances. They will assess how well educated you are, your ability to articulate your knowledge, and how you communicate.

Do you fit their perception of intelligence? Can you carry on an intelligent conversation? What have you done to better yourself? How have you developed as a result of your experiences? Is your self-directed learning ongoing and diversified? Are you dedicated to improvement? Have you searched for the necessary resources and gone through the necessary channels to evolve and grow? Are you book smart? Or street smart? Or both?

Addressing these questions on a continual basis is the key to personifying aptitude. As we move through life, we never stop learning. Change is a constant. It provides us with the opportunity to thrive, not just survive. By reading books, going to seminars, listening to tapes, CDs, DVDs, podcasts, and, above all, learning from others, we optimize our aptitude.

As this book will show, if you want to soar with the eagles, you have to hang with the eagles and ask them how they soar. The eagles are those who have achieved the lofty heights to which you aspire. Embrace them for their knowledge and perspective. They will help you get the view from above the clouds.

## Action

It's not just what you know, but what you do with what you know. Attitude and aptitude are only as good as the actions they inspire. That's why **Action** is the third and final A.

How well do you perform? Do you go the distance and beyond? How hard do you work? Do you have good habits? Do you have the discipline to take action and excel? What are your plans and goals for success? Are you committed? Are there any obstacles that would get in the way of your achieving your dreams, vision, goals, passion, and plans? What would you do to remove those obstacles?

This book will motivate you to take action, to plan your work and work your plan with timelines, goals, discipline, and flawless execution. On life's journey, you will encounter many trials and tribulations. This book explores how fear, rejection, and failure are indispensable prerequisites for success.

Action is how you will make a difference at work and to your family, your community, schools, charities, and all other areas of your life.

Your action plan must include networking, defined simply as connecting with people, people, people, and more people. And the number-one rule in networking is what I call the G7... give, give, give, give, give, give, and give again. The most successful people are the biggest givers of their time, resources, and knowledge. They share a positive, enthusiastic attitude that is contagious. Their love for what they do is pure passion. You can be sure that your efforts in networking will be reciprocated. What goes around will always circle around and find its way back to you. This book provides rules for winning the networking game.

## The Three A's Together

Here's a little story that shows the power of all three A's working in sync.

Two lumberjacks were working together. One was a veteran of 25 years and the other a strong young rookie. They were paid by the number of cords of wood they chopped each week.

The younger rookie noticed that week after week the older man's stack was always larger than his. He couldn't figure this out. After all, he was younger, stronger, and faster, and was eager to succeed. The rookie decided he would work harder and longer every day.

A few weeks passed. He started to close the gap, but still, no success.

Then one day, out of pure frustration and with blisters all over his hands, the rookie threw down his axe and went running through the forest to where the veteran was chopping. He grabbed him by the shoulder and swung him around.

"How is it that you are able to cut more wood than me every week?" he asked.

To this the veteran replied, "I've noticed that you have been working pretty hard. You have the passion, desire, dream, vision, determination, persistence, and plan, but young man, in this industry hard work and those other areas alone are not enough."

"What can I do?" the young man asked. "What's the secret?"

"There isn't any secret," the veteran said, "but there is a difference. At the end of each day, no matter how long and how hard I've worked, I always take the time to sharpen my axe. "

You have to sharpen your axe every day to realize your possibilities. This book focuses on how to do that, improving your skills and understanding in order to reach your unlimited potential.

Attitude and action were not enough for the rookie. To be as successful as the veteran, he needed the Three A's together.

By reading this book, and putting it into practice, you will tap the huge reserve of resources that you possess within you below the surface of your life. Attitude, aptitude, and action will drive success in all areas of your life.

*"And will you succeed?*
*Yes! You will indeed!*
*(98 and ¾ percent guaranteed)"*
– Dr. Seuss

When my son was sixteen, a friend asked him whether he had ever been a straight-A student. His reply was, "In grade school I had straight A's."

The friend then asked him if he was still a straight-A student. He replied, "Yes, because at the start of each school year we all start out with straight A's."

Your present needs to be your focus. You are now, at this moment, a straight-A person, student, or parent. As soon as you believe and start acting like one, you are one. The past is just experience to build from.

As my son came to realize, it's after the first few days of school that you either maintain your straight A's or settle for something less.

It all stems from your attitude and how it flows into your aptitude and how together they fuel your action.

## PART ONE

# ATTITUDE

Dream
Imagination
Belief
Confidence
Self-esteem
Vision
Acceptance
Possibilities
Eagles
Smile
Purpose
Enthusiasm
Fun
Energy
First Impression

Body Language
Love
Winners
Host
Touch, Inspire &
Move
Politely Persistent
Passion
Integrity
Failure
Rejection
Arrogance
Fear
Success Recipe
Laugh

# CHOOSE YOUR ATTITUDE

> *"It is the set of the sails, not the direction of the wind, that detemines which way we will go."*
> — *Jim Rohn*

Attitude is a big thing that makes a big difference. Life is 10% what happens to you and 90% how you react to it. It's your outlook or attitude toward circumstances and situations that will make the difference.

And, as illustrated in the book *Fish!*, by Stephen C. Lundin, Harry Paul, and John Christensen, you choose your attitude.

The authors write about Pike Place Fish Market in Seattle. Given that they are working in a fish market, most of the employees have to deal with fish guts, skins, and an awful odor. However, management and workers have decided to make their store in the market fun and their mundane and often unpleasant jobs fulfilling.

At lunchtime, crowds gather around to watch these charismatic and entertaining workers. Fish are flying all over from hand to hand as the staff do their work. Staff even get people to participate in tossing the fish around. They sing and yell that certain fish are taking off to certain parts of the country. They dance, laugh, and smile.

Many of the people who stay to watch are changed by this unique fish market. It feels good to be around positive people. They feel good, and therefore you feel good – it's contagious. And it's not bad for business either. These workers draw the biggest crowds in the market because of their positive attitude.

How is it that these workers are able to enjoy themselves in a job where most people couldn't see themselves as possibly having fun or being motivated?

The answer is attitude.

It's not the job that dictates how you feel; it's how you react to it. You choose your attitude every day. You decide the level of contribution you put into your work, and then act accordingly. The more of your heart and soul that you pour into your work, the more benefits you will reap. A positive attitude breeds positive feelings.

## Success Is a Choice

You can teach people skills. To some degree you can even teach them to think. But you cannot teach them attitude. While some people are naturally more positive or negative, ultimately they choose their attitude.

Three workers at a construction site were asked how they spent their days.

The first said, "I'm making a living."

The second said, "I'm cutting stone."

The third said, "I'm building a cathedral."

We all perceive things differently, and that perception can create a strong attitude.

> *"Happiness is not a state to arrive at but, rather,*
> *a manner of travelling."*
> *– Samuel Johnson*

---
**The one who wins is the one who thinks they can.**
---

The key to your belief and behavior is your attitude toward life. How you react through your ideas and concepts is all attitude. It doesn't matter what you choose to do in life. If you carry a positive mental attitude with you, you cannot help but be successful. What you do and what you say is important, but how you do it and how you say it is even more so.

## It's Your Choice

You may look at people doing certain jobs or certain careers and wonder how they stay focused and passionate and maintain a positive attitude. What drives their enthusiasm and their determination day in and day out? It's their attitude. That's what keeps them from getting caught in a routine, drawing in the borders of their comfort zone.

You choose your attitude every single day. If it needs to be adjusted, look inside and take responsibility. Don't blame anyone else for how you react or handle certain circumstances. You choose. It's your option.

## Attitude and Passion Make the Difference

The other day I walked into the local hamburger restaurant around the corner. George, the owner, has been at this location for 25 years. He's always smiling and obviously loves what he does. When I asked him how he feels about the McDonald's across the street, George just smiled and said, "I have my loyal customers, and business has always been steady."

"What do you mean by steady?" I asked him.

"That McDonald's franchise has been there for fifteen years," he said. "I don't do a huge business, but I am happy, and I get up every morning anxious to come to work."

George is an example of a man who has found his passion. He is content and it shows. He is rewarded by a steady business that he perceives to give him the type of living he needs and enjoys. He works long hours and by most standards doesn't make a significant amount of money. It doesn't matter. George enjoys what he does, and doesn't even consider it work.

Follow your passion and everything else will fall into place, including money, recognition, and the meaning you want in your life.

## The Attitude Equation

Attitude – it all adds up. If you assign a numerical value of 1 – 26 for each of the letters of the alphabet, Attitude = 100%.

| A | = | 1 |
|---|---|---|
| T | = | 20 |
| T | = | 20 |
| I | = | 9 |
| T | = | 20 |
| U | = | 21 |
| D | = | 4 |
| E | = | 5 |
| Grand total | | 100 |

It's our attitude that makes our life add up to 100%. This equation should be taught in all math classes!

# BELIEVE IN YOURSELF

*"If you have no confidence in self, you are twice defeated in the race of life. With confidence, you have won even before you have started."*
*– Cicero*

What gets people into the history books is being crazy enough to think they can change history. The only thing in life that can hold you back is you, so be careful what you wish!

If you make a commitment to your goal in time and persistence, it will happen. Thomas Edison believed. Henry Ford believed. Helen Keller believed. They believed in themselves.

## Play the Confidence Game

Find a successful athlete and they will speak of confidence. Find a failing athlete and they will speak of its absence. You must be optimistic. Confidence is gained with experience and success or continual success. Even the most pessimistic person can find a speck of optimism in a sand dune of failure, if they believe.

Confidence is intimately related to empowerment. It starts with setting expectations, then achieving those expectations. This in turn builds your confidence, not only in terms of how you feel about yourself but also in terms of how you feel about work, your boss, the economy, a sports team, an idea or strategy, government officials, and so on.

*"Life's battles don't always go to the stronger or faster man. But sooner or later, the man who wins, is the man who thinks he can."*
*– Vince Lombardi*

Confidence helps us take control of the circumstances around us rather than letting external forces or others' perceptions of life influence us negatively. It creates positive momentum. A lack of confidence, however, will drag us down in the game of life.

How well are you playing the confidence game?

## It Starts as a Child

Confidence and self-esteem are ingrained in us early in life. We learn from a very young age how to feel good about what we do. We receive positive reinforcement when we accomplish something, which creates a positive experience. Our surroundings help to create good habits that we carry with us the rest of our lives. Good friends who positively reinforce one another are key to creating a well-rounded, positive atmosphere for us.

Teachers also help to build this initial foundation of confidence. Your family plays a huge role as well. They contribute to a lifelong sense of self-confidence and self-esteem.

To understand where you are in life, you must recognize the factors and experiences that have influenced how you feel about yourself. Poor self-esteem rooted in a childhood experience may be turned around if you can identify the cause.

## Feeling Good About Yourself Is Contagious

If you feel good about yourself, others will feel good about you, too. First you must love yourself in order to be able to genuinely give love to others. We can be very hard on ourselves. Whenever I ask audiences, "Who is your number-one critic?" they always point to themselves.

Taking care of yourself is the greatest gift you can give to your loved ones. My wife and I always say to each other, "Please take care of you for me and I will take care of me for you." To me, this is very powerful. It is the greatest, most unselfish gift we can give.

Treat yourself as if you are your best friend, because you should be! Love yourself first and foremost if you want to extend that love and friendship to others. Who knows you better than you? Work on training your inner voice to be positive about you, repeating constructive feedback to yourself.

### Get in the Zone

Great gardeners often get in the zone when they garden because they love and believe in what they are doing. When they're in the zone, everything works and works easily, because their attitude is "I can and will succeed in planting a beautiful garden." But the same people may not be in the zone when asked to paint a picture. Why? Because that is not their passion.

Golfers who are in the zone play a round in which everything goes well, every shot is respectable or better, and they feel they can do nothing wrong. A hole-in-one, a few eagles – everything is going much better than expected.

You can even play in the zone within a zone. On a basketball team each player has an area in which they are exceptionally good. The guard can distribute and pass well and shoot very well. The center can slam dunk the ball. Just remember Michael Jordan shooting a basket to win the championship in the dying seconds of the game

You hear the phrase "in the zone" often when it comes to professional basketball. Players reflect back on playing in this way, saying, "When you are taking a shot, the basket looks huge. You just can't miss."

Take a lesson from these superstars. Believe that you are in that zone. When you truly believe in yourself, you will achieve greatness.

# LOOK IN THE MIRROR

> *"A person's worth in this world is estimated according to the value they put on themselves."*
> — Jean de la Bruyère

Your self-esteem comes down to the value you put on yourself. If you feel good about you, so will the people around you. The person you see in the mirror is the person others see based on how you feel about yourself.

In his controversial book *A Million Little Pieces*, James Frey recounts his six weeks in a drug/alcohol rehabilitation center. Frey could not look at himself in the mirror because he was ashamed of himself and what he had done. It took him a long time to finally get comfortable with the person staring back at him.

In his book he shows the lengths people will go when they just don't care about themselves or the consequences of their actions or inaction. The book is an incredible account of one man's journey to hell and back.

You can never fool the person in the mirror. That person knows what you're all about. So be honest and take responsibility. Don't blame anyone else … take responsibility for you, every day.

## Self-esteem and Performance

People who feel great about themselves expect great things of themselves. People with high self-esteem push themselves. They have tangible goals, take risks, and achieve their goals. Like Michael Jordan, they want the ball with three seconds left and the game on the line. Those with low self-worth are generally unfocused, scattered, fragile, underachieving, and lacking in discipline. They tend to avoid getting the ball at all – and they definitely don't want it when the game is on the line.

My son, Geoffrey, always says, "The best thing anybody can do better than anyone else is to be themselves." You can bring one thing that is truly unique to any situation and that is you.

This is so powerful because once you are confident with yourself and feel good about yourself, you have taken care of the first, most important element of self-confidence.

It's also important to remember that you can fool others some of the time about how you feel about yourself, but you will never be able to truly fool yourself. Deep down inside, you know how you feel. Many people have perfected wearing a mask of calmness while being a swirl of emotions inside. You will never be able to truly fool yourself about your own emotions. So get in touch with the way you feel and express it. Channel your positive emotions into your work and personal life and success will follow.

Your self-esteem, self-acceptance, self-worth, self-confidence, self-assurance, and self-respect are the foundation of your fulfillment, happiness, joy, and success. It all starts at the core, below the surface, in the huge reserve that lies within you.

## Building Esteem in Others

Another powerful way to build your own esteem is to help others build theirs. Supporting others when they are feeling low is like taking a drug to make yourself healthier. Raising the esteem of others will naturally raise your own esteem and make you feel good about yourself. Giving is the most powerful way to help yourself. The pure power of making a contribution to others works wonders. It will build within you a strong confidence in your abilities.

# THAT FIRST IMPRESSION

When you interact with someone face to face, in a meeting, at a presentation, or in a job interview, you are judged quickly on how you present yourself. Why, then, when you prepare for such meetings, do you focus on the content or "the what" of your presentation and not on "the how" of your presentation – your body language, your tone of voice, the way you come across? It would be well worth your while to actually rehearse your presentation, concentrating on the how. Professional musicians practice and rehearse for hours before they take the stage. Why should you be any different?

> **It's not just what you say, but, even more importantly, how you say it that will make or break any interaction or presentation.**

Studies show that people are most affected, in any interaction, by visual and vocal considerations. Content is important. You must know it. But how you come across visually and vocally constitutes 90% of the impression you make.

This means you should spend most of your time on the impression you give by the way you look and sound and carry yourself. Whether people decide to buy from you, engage your services, hire you, take your proposal to the next step, or even just listen to you is based on that first impression you put across.

## Windows to the Soul

In his book *How to Connect in Business in 90 Seconds or Less*, Nicholas Boothman stresses how important eye contact is in any communication.

I decided to take Boothman's teaching and test it at home. One evening I asked my children if they knew the color of their teachers' eyes. My daughter said she did. My son said he didn't. I told them that I would be meeting their teachers at parent–teacher night in a few days. I assigned them the task of confirming and relating to me the teachers' eye color before then.

My kids were used to these little tests. My son thought there should be a reward and I agreed to a dollar for every right answer. That satisfied them, but they wanted to know why I wanted this information. I said I would tell them once I had their answers.

My daughter still insisted that she already knew the answer to my question but she went through the process anyway. She was correct in every case, and I was impressed. When my son returned two days later with the results of his research, he asked me why I had given them this exercise.

I asked him, "What did you have to do to find out the color of your teachers' eyes?"

"I had to get close and look them right in the eye," he said.

His answer allowed me to teach both of them one of the key lessons of life. When you meet someone, I told them, concentrate on registering the color of their eyes. That way you will be sure to make a good connection with them.

You don't actually have to remember the color, but registering it is the right amount of time to look them in the eye and connect.

As we mature and become more experienced, it's not eye color as much as genuineness of character that we're looking for when we communicate with others. That's what is behind the expression "the eyes are the window to the soul." People's eyes will tell you whether they are genuine or not. And, thinking of it from the other side, *you* can build trust in other people when *you* look people in the eye and show your genuineness.

## Body Language

Another essential part of making a good first impression is body language. Body language is very powerful. Your physiology determines your energy and action level. If you are struggling internally with your core beliefs, your body will show the conflict.

Here's a tip: Never cover your heart. Keep your arms open, not crossed. An open gesture is warm and inviting and makes people more comfortable in communicating with you.

## Voice

First impressions aren't always just visual. Within a few seconds of a conversation, you have already been judged, on the basis of your voice, as to whether you are someone who would be enjoyable to work with or be around.

Which brings up the subject of the messages we leave on people's voicemail – and the message they hear when they call ours. Make sure *any* message you record is positive, polite, and appropriate. You want people to feel positive after hearing your voice and message.

Statistics show that in vocal communication 80% of the impression people form is based on the person's tone of voice and only 20% on the content of the message. So, to repeat: Where do you think you should be concentrating most of your preparation time, on the what or the how?

Your voicemail message represents you and your company. Here are a few ideas on how to mix it up. My voicemail message at work says, "Thank you for calling Tim Cork at NEXCareer. Please leave a detailed message, and have a great day." It is short, positive, and polite. That's the magical combination. If you call me in the month of December, you'll hear me say, "Season's greetings! Thank you for calling Tim Cork at NEXCareer. Please leave a detailed message, and have a great day." In the new year, for the month of January, you'll hear, "Happy New Year! Thank you for calling …" You get the picture.

One really interesting thing is that one in five people who leave a message pick up on the attitude behind it and close their messages with, "And you have a great day, too." It's contagious!

## Listen with All Your Senses

Listening with all your senses is an important part of making your own swift and accurate judgments about the people interacting with you. Words can be misleading. But so can body language. Sometimes words say one thing and body language says something else. When this happens, you will need to make a mental note for future reference or ask a question to clarify why the two areas aren't communicating the same message.

> *"Trust only movement. Life happens at the level of events, not of words."*
> *– Alfred Adler*

Your very presence can give reassurance to people. Your presence means you care or support them. Being there has tremendous influence and power. They appreciate having someone to bounce things off of. They appreciate your commitment of time. It's an amazing contribution to people to just listen to them.

### *Curb Appeal*

When it comes to houses, we buy based on their curb appeal. When it comes to people, we take them at face value. Looks matter. Appearances matter. Impressions are based on instinct and emotion, not on rational thought or in-depth analysis. First impressions are lasting impressions. Our experience generally proves that our first impression is usually correct. We believe our instincts and trust our gut. We can overcome the negative first impressions people have of us, but it isn't easy. It takes time for people to regain trust in us.

# DREAM BIG, REALLY BIG

> *"If you can dream it, you can do it."*
> — Walt Disney

We all need dreams to keep us going and motivated. Most of us don't dream big. The top performers and most successful people dream big. They dream about getting the home run in the bottom of the ninth, or standing on the podium receiving a gold medal at the Olympics, or being awarded the Nobel Peace Prize for humanitarian efforts.

The secret is to dream big like children. They believe there is nothing they can't do, that there are no obstacles in their way. They have no limitations on their beliefs and dreams. As adults we don't dream big enough, often enough. We believe we know better. We're realists. We've experienced the way life really is. But in fact we have been conditioned over time to believe what we can and can't accomplish.

## Goals and Dreams

Goals and dreams are totally related. Dreams are where you want to end up, and goals are the steps you take to get there.

That doesn't mean you should be unrealistic about your goals and dreams. To frame your goals realistically, you have to consider your weaknesses and opportunities for improvement. You need to adapt and strengthen those areas. Focus on the strengths, but understand how to overcome weaknesses. Be aware. Challenge yourself to create good habits.

So don't set the bar too high – but don't set it too low, either. We can always do more than we think we can, especially in chasing our dreams.

Can you imagine or see yourself in a particular role? What is your vision, your dream? What have you always wanted to do?

In the musical *Les Misérables*, Fantine, the mother of the main character, sings, "I had a dream my life would be so different / Life has killed the dream I dreamed."

While Fantine doesn't get her dream for herself, she does get a bigger and much more important dream – the dream that her daughter will get what she never had. The ultimate success in dreaming big is to dream for loved ones and others to get what they want and to help them achieve what you dream and they dream.

Another musical, *Man of La Mancha*, is about dreaming the impossible dream. What is the impossible dream that you want to accomplish?

Dreams become reality when we put them into the Straight-A's formula. Dreaming is part of our attitude. Then, through aptitude and action, our dreams can become the real thing. We have to get all three A's working for these dreams to be attainable.

Most successful people will tell you that everything they have accomplished started out as a dream. This is the seed in the imagination that grows into the tree of reality.

## Find Your Dream Team

Who are the people around you who will support you through thick and thin? Who will always be in your corner to help you, unconditionally? Serena and Venus Williams, the famous superstar tennis sisters, have spoken of how important it is for each of us to have a team around us that is always positive and on our side. As Serena put it on Oprah's show, "If they aren't part of your dream team, drop them. You don't need their negativity; you don't need them."

These two sisters have had incredible support in their dream and journey to be number one in the world. They have both achieved their dream, in the face of incredible odds. As they have found out, it's not just having the dream that matters, but having the dream team of supporters around you.

*Blank Canvas* ————————————————————————

We start every day with a blank canvas. What are you going to paint on yours? How are you going to sign it?

Every interaction starts with that blank canvas. Are people going to see a blank surface? Or are they going to see a masterpiece that makes them feel good?

Put your time and effort into being a work of art that people can get excited about.

# JUST IMAGINE...

The power of your imagination can help you do whatever you want in life. Your imagination is the center of creativity and the spark that ignites the fire of passion, belief, desire, and vision. Everything starts in the imagination. The original image is a seed. It grows as our beliefs and possibilities expand while we keep taking the right steps.

## It All Begins with Imagination

Your curiosity and interests are all born in your imagination, fueling what becomes real in your life. Your very reality is born in your imagination.

*"Imagination is more important than knowledge."*
— *Albert Einstein*

Imagination sparks knowledge. As Einstein put it, "Logic will take you from A to B. Imagination will take you everywhere else."

There are no limits to your imagination. You can go anywhere and do anything in your imagination. The key is to pull your vision, beliefs, desires, and passions out of your imagination and put them into action. Make a plan for how to achieve the goals that are lurking in your imagination. If you let yourself, you can spend most of your life in the power of your imagination.

In the Straight-A's philosophy, a positive attitude stems from the imagination. When you paint a positive image in your mind, you in turn believe and feel good about yourself, and this adds positively to any situation you are in.

To jump ahead of ourselves a bit, the Straight A's occur in combination, so imagination is part attitude and part aptitude. Without learning and education, you would not have the intelligence to understand your imagination. Then, through action, you are able to put your imagination and vision into reality.

Your imagination is that little voice inside your head that asks and wonders. That little voice that provokes you to think big, try something new, and persevere until imagination becomes real.

> *"The man who has no imagination has no wings."*
> – *Muhammad Ali*

Our imagination adjusts to the reality we have defined for ourselves through it, regardless of what is actually in front of us. Twenty people can stand in front of a piece of art and give you just as many different interpretations of the same thing. Beauty truly is in the eye of the beholder. Our senses are the gateways to our imagination and our imagination is the gateway to our lives.

Dr. Seuss summed it up perfectly in his book *Oh, the Places You'll Go!* when he said, "Think left and think right and think low and think high. Oh the thinks you can think up if only you try!"

## Do Be Childish

J.K. Rowling, the author of those incredible Harry Potter books, and Walt Disney are masters of stirring the imagination. Their mastery consists of bringing out the child in all of us.

Imagination is childlike wonderment. There are no limits when we are in a childlike state.

Isn't it amazing that young children who have just met each other can play, imagine, and have fun together as if they were lifelong friends?

## Go Anywhere!

The movie *Finding Neverland* is all about how your imagination can take you anywhere. Johnny Depp, who plays J.M. Barrie, the man who brought Peter Pan and Neverland to life, talks about turning the pages of our imaginations, about just turning the pages of our minds. "If you believe, you can go anywhere. You can go to your Neverland."

We all have our Neverland where we can go from time to time. This is an area of comfort and make-believe. We just have to believe, be happy, and have fun, to let our imaginations run wild and go to that magical place in our minds.

Our imaginations can take us over the rainbow to the Land of Oz, the Emerald City, and right back to Kansas where the adventure began. *The Wizard of Oz* impresses on our imaginations how incredibly powerful the Wizard is. Of course, we find out later that he doesn't have great powers. He does, however, have the attitude of wanting, and being able, to help anyone.

In this story, we are taken to a dream world. It makes us wish and hope for the main character, Dorothy, to realize her dream and get back to Kansas. We all want to go over the rainbow. It's the unknown. It piques our curiosity and drives us. It sparks fascination and childlike wonder in all of us.

## In Your Mind's Eye

Shakespeare used the phrase, "In my mind's eye..." Imagination is the mind's eye. It is what you see in your mind. Thoreau said, "The world is but a canvas to our imagination." We use the world as a blank canvas on which to create the masterpiece that is in our mind's eye. It is where our imaginations can manifest themselves. True masters of the imagination paint canvasses rich in all of life's splendors.

# VISION...
# THE POWER OF SIGHT

In life you need to think about where you are and where you want to be. The *want to be* part represents your dreams and is the basis of your vision. Your vision is where you want to go, your destination. You must have clarity and focus in your vision. The clearer your vision, the more successful you will be. All great and successful people are big visionaries and dreamers. The more successful you are, the bigger the dreams. To get where you want and what you want, you must visualize those destinations and achievements in every area of your life.

## The Power of Vision

As the saying goes, eyes that look are common; eyes that see are rare.

Nelson Mandela knew the power of vision. That's the only thing that kept him going during his 27-year imprisonment He has written at length about how visualization helped him maintain his sanity and positive attitude. "Over and over, I fantasized about what I would like to do," he said. "I thought continually of the day I would be free."

You should share your vision with people so you can gain support for it. Write your vision down to make it real. And keep it in front of you to review every day.

## How Visualization Works

The power of visualization consists of how your brain comes to accept what you visualize and begins to believe it to be a reality – and then begins to make it happen. Research continually shows we are much more successful in completing our goals and tasks when we visualize.

How many gold-medal athletes have said that they won by visualizing themselves standing on the podium and receiving their gold medal? Most athletes use the technique to motivate and juice their senses.

> **Vision without action = hallucination.**

That's how their vision becomes reality. Like a successful athlete, you must visualize as if you have already reached where you're heading.

Visualize your next day and how you want things to happen. Write down what you visualize. Things will have a much greater probability of happening the way you perceived them.

*"Ordinary people believe only in the possible.*
*Extraordinary people visualize not what is possible or probable,*
*but rather what is impossible. And then by visualizing*
*the impossible, they begin to see it as possible."*
– Cherie Carter-Scott

# FUEL YOUR DREAMS WITH PASSION

> *"It's time to start living the life you've imagined."*
> – Henry James

Where is your heart? The word "heart" is used in a variety of ways. Here are a few examples:

- So much comes from the heart
- From the bottom of my heart
- She wears her heart on her sleeve
- You gotta have heart
- The heart of the matter
- The heart of darkness
- Coming from the heart
- Put your heart into it
- If you open your shirt much more, your heart's going to fall out
- She has a big heart
- You're all heart

## Straight from the Heart

Often we hear the phrases "that kid's got heart" or "that person's got a heart of gold." We are conditioned to believe that the heart is a huge part of all our decisions, emotions, and reactions.

Well … it's true. Our hearts are central to everything we do. People with big hearts are considered "givers." Giving is central to getting Straight A's in life. "Straight from the heart" in its true sense means:

- Genuineness
- Passion
- Desire

- Integrity
- Conscience
- Strength

You can fool others but you can never fool yourself. Your inner self will always know where you're really coming from. What you are made up of is what it's all about. It all comes from the same source: your heart.

Trust your heart. It will never steer you in the wrong direction.

> **When you follow your heart, your feet will always be pointing in the right direction.**

## Your Heart Is Your Passion

Passion helps us achieve our goals and makes our dreams a reality. You know when someone is passionate about what they are doing. A genuine enthusiasm is ignited and comes out in every move they make or word they say. They release a powerful and often contagious energy.

Passion takes us from good to great. It helps us get excited about what we are doing or what we stand for. It's natural if we are passionate about it. Passion makes us feel comfortable and drives us to keep doing what we enjoy, helping us be the best we can be.

Passion can be your guide. Follow your passion. Believe and trust what you are passionate about. Passion is your gut instinct telling you to continue in that direction or pursuit. You can't fake it.

Tiger Woods is one of the best examples of people who have a huge heart and are driven by an incredible passion. He has an extremely rare intensity of focus, and that focus is on what he loves and believes in … golf and himself. Tiger's passion has taken him from good to great.

# IGNITE THE ENERGY WITHIN

> *"Whatever the mind can conceive and believe, it can achieve."*
> *— Napoleon Hill*

Energy is seen in the way you carry yourself. Do you exude energy and transfer it to those around you? Or do you suck it out of people? The amount of energy you give, whether positive or negative, determines how you are perceived and how you are treated.

## Positive Body Language

Your body language demonstrates energy all day long. This energy is like a chain reaction. Two positive energies build on each other to create more and more positive energy. It's like being with Oprah when she gets everyone pumped up during the taping of one her shows. The expression on her face, her stance, her posture exude confidence and enthusiasm, channeling energy to each audience member. The energy level keeps building and building as people become more excited, positive, and energized. It's the law of attraction: energy attracts energy and builds on energy.

## Words and Positive Energy

Talking positively reinforces positive energy. The effects are immediate. You can actually see people light up when they listen to someone whose words are fueled by positive energy. People have to believe in that energy and in the person who is leading or speaking. When they do, watch out!

> *"You can have anything you want if you want it desperately*
> *enough. You must want it with an inner exuberance that erupts*
> *through the skin and joins the energy that created the world."*
> *— Sheilah Graham*

Words that inspire create energy. Words accompanied by the right body language can create a genuine and contagious energy.

## Words and Negative Energy

Just as two positive energies build on each other to create more powerful energy, negative energies feed off each other, draining people of happiness, ambition, and hope. If you continually give off negative energy, people won't want to be around you. And that poses grave consequences for you in your personal and professional life.

The good news is that you can channel your negative energy into positive energy. For example, consider something you are particularly angry about, perhaps a social injustice. Your negative energy can ignite the positive energy inside people when they are persuaded by you to join your cause. The key is to get out there in the world and do something about your negative energy. Sitting around and stewing will only cause this kind of energy to fester. Being proactive will transform it into passion and a zeal for life.

## Houston, We Have Ignition!

Whether you are the receiver or the giver, take the energy that's coming through and channel it in the right direction. The energy we are talking about here is the life substance that ignites us every day.

The world and its people are one big ball of energy.

As Bob Proctor says, there's enough energy in one person to light up a small city for a week. Wow!

# RELEASE YOUR
# INNER CHILD

> *"In every real man a child is hidden that wants to play."*
> *— Nietzsche*

Kids laugh on average 400 times a day. Adults laugh an average of fifteen times a day. Why the difference? Because kids still have wonderment and spontaneity.

What happens to us adults to cause this disparity? We get so caught up in the grind and seriousness of life. We fall into our daily routines. We believe the news reports that we live in a society of doom and gloom.

Don't believe it! Be realistic about life, but then let loose and live with child-like wonder. Doing so will awaken and revive you.

## Relax!

I love acting like a child and try to understand the simple things that surround me. Take time out to observe the wonders of every day. Watch a butterfly. Imitate a monkey. Go for a walk – enjoy it, absorb it, let it flow in you. Let your hair down and relax.

> *"Don't cry because it's over. Smile because it happened."*
> *— Theodor Geisl (Dr. Seuss)*

Isn't it amazing that it's impossible to be mad when you are laughing? So laugh often. Try to laugh off the irritation or problem. Focus your thoughts on the beauty around you, maintaining that fresh, positive, genuine, childlike outlook on life.

We live in a world of abundance and marvel, miracles and beauty. Take a deep breath and let it in. Take some time every day just for you. A time where you do something you really enjoy or just sit and do nothing. It should be a time of contentment and positive thoughts.

Children see each day as their first, pure opportunity to truly live. They get excited about life and its possibilities. We need to take on a childlike spirit and review the chief lesson of childhood: that our minds create whatever we want.

Tap the childlike wonder within you ... often. It is a huge resource below the surface waiting to come out and play. The more you draw on that large reserve, the more joy, excitement, fun, happiness, and fulfillment you will attain. The boundaries are limitless.

## What Are Little Kids Made Of?

- Curiosity
- Genuine enthusiasm
- Integrity
- Innocence
- Fun
- Laughter
- Imagination
- Dreams
- No limits
- Honesty

How do we recapture these wonderful attributes that we so freely expressed when we were young and carefree?

Kevin Carroll of Nike says we lose our childlike wonder as we grow older and start to put restrictions on ourselves. These restrictions are self-inflicted and self-selected. We lose the openness and possibility of dreaming. We tend to take life and ourselves too seriously.

Kevin speaks regularly to large groups. When he asks a group of young children who among them is an artist, they all raise their hands – not just one hand but both.

When he asks adolescents, only a few raise their hands.

When he stands in front of an auditorium full of adults and asks the same question, *very few* raise a hand.

So what happens to all of us as we grow older? We lose the creativity and "artist" in all of us.

> *"Children have neither a past nor a future.*
> *Thus they enjoy the present."*
> *– Jean de la Bruyère*

If and when life gets too serious, try something out of the ordinary to have a little fun and break the pattern. Dress differently and have a little fun with it. On Halloween, dress up and have some fun. Reconnect with your inner child.

## Batman for a Day – and Forever

Thirteen years ago, on Halloween, I took my kids to school dressed as Batman. I was a big hit at their school, not only with them but also with their friends and even their teachers. After I dropped them off, I went speeding to work in my Batmobile – my black BMW. Speeding is the right word. My adrenaline was pumping and I didn't realize just how fast I was driving. A minute later, a policeman pulled me over.

As he got out of his car and started walking toward the Batmobile, he caught sight of how I was dressed. A little smile flickered across his face as he asked me to roll down the window.

"Where are you going, Batman?" he asked.

"Gotham City," I said.

"Very funny," he replied, then told me that I had been speeding and he was going to have to give me a ticket.

"Officer," I said, "I just dropped my kids off at school and everyone was so excited by how I was dressed, I guess I kind of got caught up in the moment."

The officer said he had two young kids himself. I could tell I had connected with him. Then he said, "Take off the mask."

"I'm sorry, I can't do that," I said. "I cannot reveal my identity."

"A ticket will be coming your way if you don't oblige."

I held my ground, and, fortunately, he relented. Fun and humor saved the day.

I wore the Batman suit into my office and walked around for a while before going to my office. People got a big kick out of trying to guess who was behind the mask.

That evening I got back into the costume and went trick-or-treating with my kids. They really enjoyed their dad being part of the action. When we arrived home I climbed up onto the roof and spread my wings in the moonlight, creating quite the scene for the entire neighborhood.

That costume was a real winner and the adventure was a fun time for all, especially the child in me who had a great time on holiday from the restrictions of adulthood. (I dressed up as Gumby last Halloween at work … big hit!)

Laughter helps your body and body language. It's contagious when you laugh and have fun … so lighten up. Watch a comedy, read a joke book, hang out with a friend who is funny and entertaining, tap into an outside influence that will help you enjoy yourself.

You can't stay motivated without occasional laughter. And by the way, it's good to laugh at yourself, too. Stop taking yourself so seriously. No one else is.

## "You're on Candid Camera"

Most of us light up with a smile if we think someone is taking our picture. So why not imagine that you're always on camera?

Smiles are powerful. Why do you keep going back to certain stores or restaurants? Because the staff at those places serve you with a smile. So why not think of yourself as always serving others in this pleasure-inducing way?

Do everything with a smile. A smile puts you in a positive frame of mind. Smile when you talk. Smile when you meet someone. Smiles are contagious – when you smile, people tend to smile back. Just one person smiling in a room or public place can start an epidemic of smiles. Try it sometime. Look at someone and smile. They will always smile back.

# BE ENTHUSIASTIC

> *"Enthusiasm glows, radiates, permeates and immediately captures everyone's interest."*
> — Paul J. Meyer

You must believe in what you are selling, promoting, managing, or doing and transfer this belief to the buyer. This is especially true when "the product" you are selling is yourself and the buyer is your spouse or child or friend. In fact, you are always selling yourself. Regardless of what your product or service is, people are really buying you.

Through your enthusiasm, you can be effective. If you are feeling good about yourself and your product, you will be successful. However, showing excessive enthusiasm or false enthusiasm is a quick way to turn people off. Enthusiasm must be sincere. When it is, real energy will be released. Your motive will be apparent.

## Genuine Enthusiasm

Enthusiasm is derived from the Greek word "enthousiasmos," which means inspiration.

People perceive it in a flash if you don't mean what you say or your body language isn't in harmony with your words. Most of us are open books. It's easy for people to detect whether we really mean what we say.

Anyone with genuine enthusiasm definitely inspires us.

Children's enthusiasm is almost always genuine. They can turn it on immediately. They don't have to be prompted or pretend. We adults tend to hesitate because we feel silly or it just doesn't feel natural. We need to keep in mind that we don't get that second chance to create a first impression.

## The Key Ingredient

Enthusiasm is the key to all winning teams and successful businesses. Enthusiasm attracts us like a magnet. It creates motivation, helping us overcome fear, rejection, and failure. It is a big part of courage and burning desire, the fire in the gut that drives us.

Enthusiasm is a big part of attitude and getting Straight A's in life. Without this crucial ingredient, you will never achieve the success you desire.

I like Henry Ford's fireplace motto:

*You can do anything if you have enthusiasm.*
*Enthusiasm is the yeast that makes your hope rise to the stars.*
*Enthusiasm is the sparkle in your eye,*
*it is the swing in your gait, the grip of your hand,*
*the irresistible surge of your will, and your energy to execute your ideas.*
*Enthusiasts are fighters.*
*They have fortitude. They have staying qualities.*
*Enthusiasm is at the bottom of all progress!*
*With it is accomplishment. Without it there are there are only alibis.*

# LOVE CHANGES EVERYTHING

> *"There are many things in life that will catch your eye.*
> *But only a few will catch your heart. Pursue those."*
> — Ben Crenshaw

The movie *A Beautiful Mind* tells the story of the brilliant mathematician John Forbes Nash (played by Russell Crowe). In the ceremony, in 1994, in which he receives the Nobel Prize in Economic Sciences for breakthroughs in game theory earlier in his career, he thanks his wife for giving him the strength to get through the trials and tribulations he experienced during years of mental illness.

In the end, it was love, more than theoretical brilliance, that really mattered. It's the power of love that endures. Nash was able to persevere because of his wife's unconditional love and support. Perhaps she should have received a Nobel for what *she* did.

## All You Need Is Love

Love is the most powerful emotion we have. It is the heart that makes the final decision. It is the heart that ultimately influences every action. Like the 90% of the iceberg that's below the surface, giving the iceberg its power, it's the heart that truly impacts and affects our actions. The heart keeps us going and drives our attitudes and actions.

How do you love your family, your work, and most importantly yourself? Are you happy with each of these areas of your life? Love is the driving force that leads us down certain paths every day of our lives. Some of the paths are a test of our love and belief systems. Some are parts of the journey that enlighten and strengthen us.

You could write about love for pages until you've spun those words into chapters and then into a whole book. It has been done before. The key is that love is in all of us to share. When we can give more and it is unconditional, we are tapping what's below the surface of our own lives, where a large reserve of strength exists.

In the Dr. Seuss tale *How the Grinch Stole Christmas*, the Grinch has a change of heart after he realizes that Christmas isn't just about presents.

*"And what happened then ... ?*
*Well ... in Who-ville they say*
*That the Grinch's small heart*
*Grew three sizes that day!"*

The Grinch discovered what he was really all about: simply put, that love conquers all, and that giving this love to others is what the holidays are all about.

## Love Unconditionally

There is no reward greater than giving unconditional love. It's in you to give.

I wear a bracelet every day – one of the ones my daughter, Stephanie, has given me – because they remind me of my goal to keep my perspective no matter what happens to me, and because the love they represent is what helps me keep my perspective and achieve balance in life.

It all started when Stephanie was into beading as a young girl. Not surprisingly, this was inspired by years of arts and crafts at Taylor Statten Camps, which she attended in the summers.

When she was nine years old, she presented me with a bracelet that had beads on a fishing line. The bracelet said, "Dad, I love you," and had two happy faces on it. Out of curiosity, I asked her, "What are the happy faces for?" – thinking she had put them on because of the colors: pink and purple were her favorites. I assumed they had no meaning.

Not so. "That's me and Geoffrey smiling at you," she replied. "Whenever you want to feel good, all you have to do is look at your bracelet."

Wow! She asked me if I would wear it, and I said, "Every day."

So every year, she would make me a different bracelet, saying "Dad, I love you" or some variation on that wonderful theme.

However, she slowly outgrew this phase and eventually stopped making the bracelets. On request, she made me a leather bracelet, which is one of the bracelets I often wear.

Once, early in this tradition, I told her that I sometimes had to roll a bracelet up my sleeve because it would look inappropriate when I was with a customer. You know what her reply was?

"You should let the bracelet show even in business situations," she said, "because you might be speaking to customers who have kids themselves and this would give you common ground for your conversations."

I was blown away by this comment, and I have followed her advice. When I'm talking to a customer who has kids, I will tell the story of Stephanie and her

> **What's your anchor to remind you of what's most important in your life?**

bracelets. This helps the customer to see me as a human being, not just a salesperson.

She gave me a bracelet two years ago that says 12/26/04. This is a very significant date. It's the day the tsunami hit in Indonesia, deeply affecting people around the world. On the other side of the bracelet it says, "Give Love," with a red cross beside it. I wear it on my wrist every day. It reminds me that the most powerful way to deal with tragedies is to give love to all those affected. And it reminds me of my daughter's love for those in trouble.

## What's in It for Me?

> **Say those three little words to the ones you love – "I love you." Then say, "All I want, all I ask, all I need is you."**

When you give love, you get what you give. Zig Ziglar talks about how he and the Redhead (his wife) always exchange hugs. They can never get enough. Hugging is such a great way to express love and admiration. It's nice to touch that special someone. A hug of gratitude and thanks goes a long way. A hug of appreciation and warmth is very powerful.

## What Do You Love?

People are good at what they love. Passion drives us to do what we love, whether we're at work or play.

> *"Find something you love to do and you'll never have to work a day in your life."*
> *– Harvey Mackay*

Make a list of 10 to 20 things you love or love doing. Then make sure that what you put on that list is the foundation of everything you do in life. If you don't love what you are doing and where you are, then make a change.

## The Love List

I love _____

I love _____

I love _____

I love _____

I love _____

I love _____

I love _____

We can only truly excel at what we love to do. We can only be happy if we do these things with the ones we love in our personal life. My list has a few people like my wife, my kids, my mother. Also getting on my list are writing, reading, hockey, public speaking, giving, and canoe trips. I make sure I include these in every part of my life.

> *"I believe that the very purpose of our life is to seek happiness."*
> – Dalai Lama

I take inventory on a regular basis to guarantee that these people and things and experiences are getting the lion's share of my time and energy. Do an inventory of your life. Are you spending the majority of your time doing what you love?

## A Love Story

Larry King said *The Notebook* was the greatest love story he had seen in years. If you're going to watch it, get out the Kleenex first, because this movie will take you on a roller coaster of emotion. The passion of the two main characters in the movie and the depth to which their story will take your senses are extraordinary. Love is not easy, but it is pure and worth the effort when the perfect mate enters your life. This is the person you most want to be with, regardless of circumstances. In fact, the inevitable tests of life only serve to strengthen your bond.

Both of the main characters, Noah and Allie, know the other will always be there. They both have total, unconditional love for each other. Nothing can break this bond. One of the characters gets dementia and writes the notebook so the other character can bring back good memories as the terrible disease takes its toll. Another major barrier that proves no match for Noah and Allie's love.

Early in the movie, when they first meet, Noah learns from Allie that painting is one of her true loves. Noah goes to great lengths to enable her to have a studio and do what she loves. True love is helping your soul mate do what they love to do. Noah is happy when Allie is happy doing what she loves to do.

## Your Sixth Sense

Love is a sixth sense that combines the senses to create the feelings that are timeless. Love comes from the heart, soul, and mind. When you find that special someone, nothing can get in your way. Love conquers all.

You can only excel and have true passion doing what you love to do. One of the greatest gifts you can give, therefore, is to help others find and live their passions in life.

# FORGIVE AND ACCEPT

> *"Only by acceptance of the past, will you alter its meaning."*
> – T. S. Eliot

Some of the most important actions we can take are of a personal nature. A true story from my own life illustrates one of these actions: asking for forgiveness and moving on beyond that to acceptance.

There is a big difference between forgiveness and acceptance. Acceptance takes forgiveness to the next level. It frees you and enables you to move forward. After forgiving someone, you may still be affected by feelings of hurt, caging up those emotions for years. Without acceptance, you will not move forward. In fact, if you have forgiven someone but have not accepted that person and accepted what happened to you, moving on from it, have you really forgiven at all?

## A Weight off My Shoulders

For approximately 35 years I had harbored deep resentment toward my father. He left our home when I was twelve and seemed to disappear from my life. I could not understand why he never made an effort to be part of my life or the lives of my siblings. He remarried and started a second family, leaving my mother to raise three boys on her own. What really disappointed me was watching my mother soldier on alone when I knew she should have had help from my dad.

I didn't know what to do except to blame him. I was angry at him for letting us down, for not caring about us. There were years when I refused to see or even speak to him.

But something happens to us as we age. We begin thinking about our lives and the circumstances or defining moments of our lives. Increasingly, I found myself analyzing and pondering my relationship with my father and its effect on how I turned out.

When I was young I vowed that if I ever had a family of my own, I would always be there for my kids. My brothers must have made the same promise to themselves, judging by how attentive they are to their families.

Last year I took a course that helped me understand and break through my feelings. This course taught me about acceptance. One of the exercises was to write a letter, just for our own reflection. I chose to write to my dad.

As I did so, I decided to act on it. I had not seen my father for five years. I had only spoken to him a few times during that time, and had decided that I didn't really care if I ever saw him again. I figured the next time I would see him would be at his funeral.

> *"Home is where hearts open and forgiveness and acceptance are the rule."*
> *– Kall*

In the morning, on day two of this three-day course, the leader of the course called me up in front of the group of about 200 people and asked me to share my letter with them. I told them my story. Getting this pain and resentment off my chest was a breakthrough for me. So was promising the people in front of me that as a result of the course I was going to visit my father and put my acceptance into action.

## An Interesting Path

This was no easy exercise. This particular call to action led me down an interesting path; a path I was not comfortable with. I feared where it might lead. I had to find my father and then meet him and have the most intimate conversation with him that we ever had. At the time, I didn't even know where he was. I then learned that my father was in prison for spousal abuse. I also didn't know the woman he had been living with.

I went to see my father, in prison, which was located a little over two hours by car from where I live. When I arrived at the prison, I signed in, walked through long cold hallways, took an elevator down two floors, went through two more guard stations, and finally sat down on a hard plastic chair behind a clear plastic wall.

My father was escorted in by a guard and sat down face to face with me. It was a shock for me to see him looking every bit the prison inmate that he was, wearing the standard-issue orange jumpsuit. One side of me saw him as caged and helpless and somehow not deserving of all this. Another side of me knew he did deserve to be there.

Dad had aged tremendously. I barely recognized him, and he didn't recognize me, at first. When he figured out who I was, a tear rolled down his cheek and then one rolled down mine as we stared at each other for what seemed like an eternity.

Finally, we picked up the phones and talked. I told him I had come not to forgive him, but to thank him for all the good things he had done for me and given me. I told him that I loved him and then said goodbye. It was short, but it brought closure to a huge part of my life. I realized that this was probably the last time I would ever see my dad.

I hate to think what would have happened to me if I had allowed my feelings of disappointment to spill over into another decade of my life.

Three days later, the course reconvened and an additional 500 people joined us in a large ballroom at the hotel. I was called up by the leader to tell my story. I was asked how this course had impacted me. I spoke to the crowd about how it had helped me go above and beyond forgiveness to acceptance.

I had gone so long never intending to dig up my past with my father and the deep pain I felt, and now here I was telling this very personal story to this large group.

I shared with them for two reasons. The first was for the therapeutic effect and closure for me. The second was to help others confront their fears and demons and empower them to take action and achieve closure. This is also why I am sharing it with you. My attitude was totally changed because of this experience. My perspective changed. I went deep and tapped into strengths far below the surface.

Is there an area in your life requiring closure? Forgiveness is a powerful first step, but acceptance will take you to the next level and give you the closure required. This gift and life-changing experience in my life were the result of my continuous thirst to learn and study. I took this course to learn some new concepts and ideas. It turned out to serve a much greater purpose, helping me explore and take on a hurt I didn't want to face.

Life's learning never stops; there are many pieces to your puzzle.

I know my father has done many wonderful things in his life and made a difference to many people, including me. I want to remember the good effect he had on me and accept him unconditionally. Though I may not comprehend or agree with his actions, he is who he is and I will always love him.

The most important acceptance in our lives is our own personal acceptance of ourselves. It is not easy to accept ourselves in all we do. We doubt our thoughts and actions every day. When we can get to the mountain top of accepting those around us, we can move up the higher mountain of accepting ourselves for who we are.

## Carpe Diem – Seize the Day!

The present is what you can control, so be present in the present. Not just by being there physically but also by staying focused in the present mentally. Acceptance of what happened to me in the past helped me learn from the past and move on to live more fully in the present. And, of course, the experience of acceptance changed my entire future.

# BE THE HOST

> *"You can have everything in life you want*
> *if you will just help enough other people get what they want."*
> *– Zig Ziglar*

When you are the host of a party or event, you play a very definite role. You carry yourself a certain way and act a certain way. When people arrive, you make sure they feel welcome, that they meet others, that they get a drink and something to eat. When you are a guest, your attitude is totally different. You tend to look for your comfort zone and hang with people you know. Sometimes you may spend the whole evening in that comfort zone because it's the easy thing to do.

> **My challenge to you is be the host every day!**

> *"A guest never forgets the host who had treated him kindly."*
> *– Homer*

An excellent way for you to develop your communications skills is to deal with people, whether in a one-to-one situation or in a group, as if you are the host. It doesn't matter whether you're doing business in a formal setting or standing with others in an elevator. When you are the host, you are focused on others and their comfort. Rare is the human being who does not love being treated this way.

Now, the idea of being the host of course does not mean that you should feel free to take over an event or someone else's party. Being the host is the personification of an attitude, an attitude that helps people feel at ease. People will feel comfortable with you. They will be drawn to you because your confidence breaks down barriers between people, helping them feel good about themselves and encouraging them to open up to others. After all, you are leading by example as you introduce yourself to others and them to still others. Your genuine enthusiasm is the catalyst that ignites a warmth that keeps on flowing throughout the duration of the event or party. As people catch the feeling you are promoting, their mood, and the mood of the group as a whole, is elevated.

## A Host

- Introduces people
- Exudes confidence
- Leads by example
- Is the catalyst
- Is proactive, moving around
- Helps you out
- Has a positive outlook
- Circulates/networks
- Helps those not in their comfort zone

## A Guest

- Moves to those they already know
- Is more reactive than proactive
- Follows the crowd
- Doesn't want to be the host
- Stays out of the spotlight
- Takes the easy road
- Cruises in mediocrity

# BE POLITELY PERSISTENT

*"Politeness wins the confidence of princes."*
— Chinese proverb

You will always go further and gain more respect when you are politely persistent.

It's true that people who succeed are persistent. But impolite persistence does not lead to success – at least not to lasting success. Some people lack tact and their persistence is simply rudeness. That's not the kind of persistence I'm talking about. Annoying others through pure aggressiveness won't get you anywhere – or anywhere you want to be. You may gain a short-term win or your perception of a win, but life is not a sprint, it's a marathon. Polite persistence will always win the race.

## The Power of Politeness

Polite persistence is using empathy to understand and appreciate the other's point of view and why they may feel a certain way and then working to ensure a win-win solution for both sides.

There is no reason not to be polite. Being polite to polite people is good – it's the basis of everyday civility. But being polite to rude people is much more powerful and leads to personal success in many ways.

Success happens as a result of how you treat others. How are you acting? Are you consistent in the way you treat others?

## True Politeness

There is a thin line between being confident and being arrogant. When people are impolite, it is usually because they are arrogant or believe they are above others. No one has earned the right to be impolite. As long as you are polite when you are trying to get in touch with someone or get them to return your calls, you can be persistent. What are they going to say to you, "Stop calling and being so polite to me"? As long as you are genuine, then true politeness ensures that everything will fall into place.

Adults love it when children are polite. "Please" and "thank you" are always welcome and should be used as often as possible.

# BE CONFIDENT, NOT ARROGANT

> *"Arrogance invites ruin; humility receives benefits."*
> – Chinese proverb

Some people think they are entitled to act arrogant. But this attitude is never acceptable. No one has ever earned that right.

## The Arrogance Disease

Arrogance can kill an individual and an organization. The more arrogant people act, the less successful they will be in the long run.

The formula is: arrogance = insecurity. Arrogance promotes an "it's all about me" attitude. Arrogance is a disease that creeps in and destroys. There is no "giving" in arrogance, just the desire to get at the expense of others.

## The Difference Confidence Makes

Where arrogance drives people away, confidence draws them in. People are attracted to genuine people who feel good about themselves. Try it and you will see that when you are genuine and confident, the world will get onside with you and everyone, including you, will feel good about you.

In my business of career transition/outplacement, the arrogant and the confident fall into two very different camps.

The arrogant, though they need a new career or a new job, resist my help, at least initially. They are sure they can make it on their own.

The confident are happy to have help.

When people tell me they don't need help, I pull out this little statement: "The only reason anyone in your situation would consider going it alone is ignorance, arrogance, or both."

The statement is meant to shock, and it usually does. People look at me as if I shouldn't be so direct. I respond by saying that I think they are intelligent people and then ask, "Why would you try to do it by yourself when you can work with a team of experts?" – simply meaning that the power of the group is always greater than the power of the individual, and that thinking otherwise is pure arrogance.

Most get it, but there are some who are either too arrogant to understand what I'm saying, or too proud to admit that I'm right.

People with a Straight-A attitude will admit when they don't know something and ask for help. If you think you are too good for someone else's help, consider taking the path from arrogance to confidence. It can be a tough path to travel, but it's worth it.

> *"Whoever undertakes to set himself up as a judge of Truth and Knowledge is shipwrecked by the laughter of the gods."*
> *– Albert Einstein*

# HOW RUDE!

I wish a little note would pop up on the screen of those pocket computers and phones people are fond of fiddling with when they get together. The note would say, "Wow, are you ever important. The rest of us obviously are not."

## Sad Scenes

When you are with someone, whether at lunch or in a meeting, you should focus on them. Checking your schedule or taking or making a phone call is rude and goes against the principle of "being present" with people.

Cell phones, beepers, BlackBerries, and other hand-held devices are wonderful inventions. If they are used right, they can increase your productivity exponentially. However, when people in a meeting or social situation leave them on and then say, "Excuse me while I get this," they are showing total disregard for the others around them.

Here's one of the saddest little scenes of modern life: two people strolling down the street while each is speaking to someone else on their cell phone. We are in danger of losing common courtesy and our ability to communicate face to face.

## A Means of Escape?

Is this behavior an excuse to get away from something or even to absent oneself from the present? These communications devices should be used as they were meant to be used. When they aren't, they become tools of arrogance.

Here are some perfectly acceptable ways to respond to these situations. You could say, "Please put that down and let's just talk face to face." Or "Maybe we should talk some other time when you are able to communicate with me."

Our priorities are transparent when we allow ourselves to be monopolized by these devices in front of others. Know when to turn them off. You are just not that important – and the person with you is!

# INTEGRITY ...
# IT'S ALL OR NOTHING

> *"If you tell the truth you don't have to remember anything."*
> *— Mark Twain*

Follow the path of integrity and you will never get lost. It is like Dorothy in *The Wizard of Oz* following the yellow brick road to the Emerald City. It is a path of innocence, protection, and a means to get back home. Integrity is the path of life.

Integrity flows from self-knowledge. Without integrity, you are not going to be successful.

Integrity is the Three A's covered in this book – attitude, aptitude, and action – singing in perfect harmony. People spot that you are a person of integrity when they perceive your positive, confident attitude, see that you are capable of doing what you say you're going to do, and then see that you in fact did do what you promised.

## Integrity Is Genuine

There's something odd about integrity. People can't give it to us and they can't take it from us. It's up to us to earn it and it's our choice alone whether we lose it. Those who get Straight A's in attitude, aptitude, and action make a success out of life because other people are attracted to their ideas and causes – and integrity.

You either have 100% integrity or 0% integrity. Integrity is an all-or-nothing game. Can you imagine saying of someone, "That person is a person of 50% integrity"?

## Two Shining Examples of Integrity

I work with a man named Jeff who personifies integrity in everything he does. Jeff is a true giver and spends most of his free time helping people. Jeff spends countless hours with less fortunate kids and the homeless. Through his positive attitude, he helps them feel better. This motivation is also a big part of his work as a life and career coach. He helps others discover their strengths and feel good about themselves.

When you meet Jeff he is always positive. He is as genuine as it gets, which is the key ingredient of integrity. Jeff's values and principles are always in line with his actions, which personify honesty, goodwill, and integrity. I enjoy just being around Jeff to have some of his magic rub off on me. He is always smiling, and that is contagious, too.

Another person who exudes integrity is Wayne Gretzky. Wayne is an individual who has had incredible success in all areas of his life and is a role model of the Straight-A's person. He has never let his fame and fortune go to his head and is always a giver in everything he does. Like Jeff, he spends a large amount of his time working for charities and donating his time to help others. Wayne always seems to be doing the right thing. Because of his integrity, he attracts success.

# GET RIGHT BACK UP

> *"I get knocked down*
> *But I get up again*
> *You're never going to keep me down."*
> *— Chumbawamba*

If you get knocked down, how quickly do you get back up? The adage of falling off a horse and getting right back into the saddle is true. The difference between successful and unsuccessful people is how they react to falling.

## An Example of Fortitude

Christopher Reeves wasn't so fortunate. He was paralyzed when he fell off his horse. But, in his own way, he did get right back up. His fortitude in dealing with his paralysis and raising funds for others suffering from spinal-cord injuries made us all proud. It helped us realize what a positive attitude and unwavering belief can do when tragedy strikes.

> *"Great works are performed not by strength, but by perseverance."*
> *— Samuel Johnson*

What an ironic twist when "Superman" becomes vulnerable and is hit by tragedy, only to rise up again as a true-to-life hero, winning the hearts of millions. What an inspiration and role model of what people are capable of when life knocks them down. He helped us realize that the superman in all of us is how we react and go head-to-head with life's incredible tests.

### An Ant's Life

Ants think winter all summer. What an incredible attitude! They collect food in the warm months so they can live through the hardship of the cold months.

How much will ants gather? As much as they can. They know that the winter will not be postponed, so they are not lured away from their task. They understand something that we should understand: that you can't compete with Mother Nature.

When you get a chance to watch some ants, take some time and watch them closely. You will learn a lot about hard work, determination, persistence, and a positive attitude.

Our lives are like the seasons. Each season brings its own kind of beauty and bounty. But each season can also bring challenges and hardship. A can do, positive attitude makes all the difference in how we weather the seasons of our lives.

# FEAR...FRIEND OR FOE?

> *"Our doubts are traitors, and make us lose the good*
> *we oft might win by fearing to attempt."*
> *– Shakespeare*

Is fear our enemy or friend? I believe it can be either – it just depends on our attitude.

Your attitude toward fear probably stems from your childhood and how your parents modeled their own perceptions of fear. They may have protected you from fear. Or they may have caused fear. Sometimes all it takes is contradictory treatment by otherwise loving parents to destabilize us into a fearful existence. When we receive mixed signals, confusion sets in.

Out of frustration and a clear lack of direction, some of us grow up to embrace drugs or alcohol to shield us from reality. Call it chemical courage.

What should you do when you come up against something you fear? You must have the courage to face it head on. Learning from it is the only way to escape the fate of having to face it over and over again.

## Dealing with My Own Fear

It's well known that public speaking is one of people's greatest fears. Some fear it more than death, according to some surveys.

I'm a public speaker by profession, so you would think that I have always been a natural at it. Nothing could be further from the truth.

Every time I speak in front of an audience I get a little nervous. It's good nerves. I am pumped up and excited, but always a little anxious about the first impression I will make. The day I don't get nervous is the day I shouldn't be doing it anymore, because that's when arrogance will have taken the place of confidence.

I used to be a real sweater in front of crowds. The sweating subsided once I learned, over time, to pause, drink lots of water, and get more comfortable with my material.

I also like to move around a lot when I speak. Once, two minutes into a speech, in front of 300 people, I stepped right off the stage and landed in the crowd! Now, for my own survival if nothing else, I have learned to take a breath, focus, and consciously slow my movements down.

When it comes to your fears, you need to take control. Don't just let things happen – move beyond your fear. The fear that you let build up in your mind is worse than the situation that actually exists. In the absence of confidence, fear and worry take control. Fear breeds doubt and doubt leads to lack of confidence.

The secret is to go headfirst into your fears while visualizing a successful outcome, if not this time, then maybe the next. Keep at it. That will help you beat the fear. You will then gain momentum and gain confidence. Once you've done it enough and you believe that you are self-confident, people will begin to react to your confidence. As you exhibit the comfort you feel from defeating the demons that were playing on your doubts, you will gain self-control and success will begin to become a normal part of your life.

A great way to face fear is to set your body in motion. Walk, roller blade, run, swim, golf, cycle. Give yourself time to think and reflect – time with no interruptions and no interference. This will enable you to confront challenges with an open mind.

When your body is in motion, it will add to your energy, power, and direction. It will create positive stimuli to help you generate ideas and solutions. Fear can help us put things in perspective, enabling us to think more clearly about what we should do when we come face to face with fear again.

### *Be an Artist*

Think of great artists like Da Vinci, Van Gogh, and Picasso. They headed right into their fears. By taking risks they moved up to the next level in their art.

In a way, they not only faced the unknown, they created it. And by not following the crowd, they created crowds. Just think of the people milling in front of their masterpieces at art museums all over the world.

## Fighting Fear

Firefighters deal with fear every time they prepare to go into a burning building. They deal with the uncertainty of not knowing whether they'll come out alive. What's their secret?

They step into their fear – literally. They hit it head on. Then they shift into being 100% in the present moment. This allows them to do all the things they were trained to do, in a sense without thinking. By facing fear, they can focus on the immediate situation and get the job done.

Ask any firefighter whether fear plays a big role in their work and they will always tell you yes. They will then tell you that they are trained to face fear and do their job in the face of that fear in order to save lives.

Think about it. When everyone else is running out of a burning building, firefighters are just as urgently running into it. During 9/11, hundreds of firefighters ran into the towers as everyone else was desperately trying to get out. Their courage has helped put fear in perspective for the rest of us.

You can tap the iceberg of other people, too. You can tap the huge emotional reserve below the surface to really affect them and have a true impact on them. When you do this with precision and perfect timing and then channel the emotions in the right direction, you are serving as a powerful catalyst in their lives.

The best movies, books, plays, and music take us on an emotional roller coaster ride, which is why we remember them. Your impact on people is a result of the emotion you are able to evoke. Your ability to touch, inspire, and motivate people will drive a positive response and stir their emotions.

## *Ride the Roller Coaster*

> *"Life can be like a roller coaster ... and just when you think you've had enough, and you're ready to get off the ride and take the calm, easy merry-go round ... you change your mind, throw your hands in the air and ride the roller coaster all over again. "*
> – *Stacey Charter*

Not only can fear be our friend, but our other emotions can be, too. This doesn't immediately make sense, because emotions tend to overrule logic and take us places we shouldn't go. Emotions come from the heart and shoot through our whole body, often causing us to make rash decisions in what we buy, where we go, and who we're with. However, it is possible for us to channel our emotions into positive energy.

If you really want to make a difference, play to people's emotions. When people realize you really care, their emotions override everything else. Make it emotional for them: get them to where emotion is driving the decision.

# CHOOSE YOUR BEHAVIOR

> *"Insanity is to keep doing the same thing in the same way and expect a different outcome."*
> – Chinese proverb

The behavior you choose creates your results. You would think that repeating the behavior would make you comfortable with the results. But often it doesn't. We are caught in a Bill Murray *Ground Hog Day* of repetition and want to get out.

## Changing Behavior

The solution is to think the other way, to realize that to change the outcome you must change your behavior. That alone is the beginning of substantial progress. Understanding how to eliminate behavior that is taking you down an unproductive, self-destructive road will help improve your life.

You can do this in two ways. One is to stop behaving in the negative; the other is to start behaving in the positive.

> *"People are always blaming their circumstances for what they are. I don't believe in circumstances. The people who get on in this world are the people who get up and look for the circumstances they want, and, if they cannot find them, make them."*
> – George Bernard Shaw

To change your behavior, you must change your attitude. What happens on the outside does not have to be what you feel on the inside. You control your reactions, and must adjust accordingly

## Perfect Practice Makes Perfect

Getting better is not just a matter of practicing the same thing again and again. In some instances that will cause you just to get better at the bad habit you had in the first place.

Tiger Woods always says that practice isn't the only ingredient. His formula is that perfect practice makes perfect. He is the best in the world, yet he still has coaches continually working with him on his game. He is better than any of his coaches but knows he needs the help of other experts to keep at the top of his game.

If you continue what you are doing and you are just getting better at your bad habits, you need to ask or engage an expert to help you learn and understand the right way to excel. Don't practice your bad habits; seek to develop good habits and practice them perfectly.

## *You vs. You*

Golf is a good example of changing behavior. In golf you are trying to beat your best score each and every time. You are competing against others but only as you compete against yourself in your quest to become better.

This concept of you vs. you is the outlook you should always have. If you remember that you are in this game of life to continually improve yourself, you will always come out on top. In the game of life you need to concentrate on beating your last score.

# WINNERS VS. LOSERS

> *"Losers make promises they often break.*
> *Winners make commitments they always keep."*
> – Denis Waitley

To be a winner you must have a winner's attitude. Here are a few of the ways winners look at life and a few ways losers see it:

## Winners

- See themselves as part of the answer
- Always have a solution, are part of the solution
- Say, "Let me do it for you!"
- See answers for every problem
- See the green near every sand trap
- Admit it's difficult but believe it's possible
- See the glass as half full
- See the light at the end of the tunnel
- Experience cloudy days as silver days
- Translate "mountain" into "opportunity and challenge"
- Follow through
- Are accountable and admit mistakes
- Make it happen
- Believe in win/win
- Fall forward

## Losers

- Are part of the problem
- Always have an excuse
- Say, "That's not my job!"
- See a problem for every answer

- See two or three hazards for every fairway
- Agree it may be possible but believe it's difficult
- See the glass as half empty
- Believe the light at the end of the tunnel is a train
- Experience silver days as cloudy days
- Translate "opportunity and challenge" as "mountain"
- Expect to lose
- Blame others
- Quit
- Believe in win/lose
- Fall backwards

*"Winners expect to win in advance.*
*Life is a self-fulfilling prophecy."*
*– Anonymous*

# PURPOSE... THE BIG "WHY"

When you have a purpose, everything falls into place. Your purpose is what's important to you. It drives you, it is your passion for doing what you love to do, it is what motivates you. Everyone must have a purpose. What is yours? What is the big "why" that drives you to do what you do?

I use my name, TIM, as an acronym to remind me of my purpose: to Touch, Inspire, and Move people to act on their passion and goals. The C in my last name, Cork, stands for Catalyst, because I want to help make this happen.

This is the guide for everything I do. This is my big why, my passion and motivation every day. It gives my life purpose. Purpose is the compass that keeps me pointed in the right direction, toward true north, as Stephen Covey would say. Why not have your own simple acronym to remind you of your purpose?

## Where Are You Going?

You must have a big enough why to keep you interested in the direction you are headed. The why is your path to success. Why are you here on this planet called earth? Be clear and be precise about this.

How you feel at any time will tell you whether or not you are living your purpose. When you are acting in ways that line up with your purpose, you will feel an inner joy. It's a joy that's almost addictive. Because you want to keep feeling it, you want to stay within your purpose.

> **Find your cause.
> What drives you?**

When I touch, inspire, and move people, it helps them accomplish their goals and feel better about their possibilities in the direction they want to go. It makes them feel better about themselves, which in turn gives them the awareness and self-confidence that they are capable of achieving anything they want in life. They understand that through a Straight-A's philosophy, there are no limits.

# UNCORK YOUR POSSIBILITIES

> *The universe is full of magical things, patiently waiting for our wits to grow sharper."*
> – Eden Phillpotts

My wife, Suzy, gave me a bottle that says "Uncork Your Possibilities" on the front. It is a small bottle that is hand painted with sunshine and beautiful colors. When she gave it to me, she told me it had special power – that whenever I opened it and poured the invisible ingredients on my head, good things would happen, if only I believed.

## Say Yes to the Magic Elixir

The idea came to her when she saw an amazing man named Kevin Carroll speak to a group of 5,000 people. He had his own bottle on the stage. He offered it to anybody in the audience who wanted to come up and pour some of the special ingredients it contained on their heads. Most people were skeptical and reluctant. Many saw it as silly.

When you make this offer to a group of children, they jump right up and volunteer. They have the creativity and imagination to immediately deal with this and explore the unlimited possibilities through their minds.

> **I hope you never lose your sense of wonder.**

What happens to us as adults? We question our possibilities and beliefs and get stuck in a rut.

Next time someone offers you a bottle with a magic elixir in it or an opportunity to explore through your imagination, don't hesitate. Let your childlike wonder take over and take you to those places you always wanted to go.

## Let the Dreams Take Over

I use my bottle with audiences from time to time and they respond slowly at first, and then, when it seems safe or others start the ball rolling, they jump in.

Pour a little on you, and then let the dreams and possibilities take over.

What's your magic bottle? Take the time to really think and let your mind wander into the areas of your dreams, beliefs, and vision. There are no boundaries in your imagination, so put no boundaries on where you go.

PART TWO

# APTITUDE

Proof = Credibility

Testimonials

Mentors

Kindergarten

Dr. Seuss

Ducks & Eagles

Be the Teacher

Change

Journals

Read the Books

Juice the Senses

Experience

Perception & Reality

Precious Present

Everyone Is a Customer

Knowledge

Power

Listen

Quality & Quantity

Mastermind Concept

# WHAT WE LEARN
# IN KINDERGARTEN

We have traveled together through the A of attitude. Now it is time to move on to the A of aptitude: what we are learning, what we can do, how we can apply our attitude and skills in readiness for putting them into action (which is the third A and the focus of Part Three of this book).

Most of what we need to know we learn by the time we graduate from kindergarten. We learn that people can and will say just about anything and they have no sense of tact at times. That there are leaders among us, followers, bullies, smart people, athletic people, aggressive people, well-meaning people, along with not so well-meaning people. The list goes on and on.

## It Starts Young

Making choices and decisions starts at a very young age. Failure, rejection, and fear, as well as other emotions, are everywhere around us. Starting in those tender years from three to five, we learn about hurt. If we have the right people around us, we learn early that fear, failure, and hurt are all part of growing up and that these experiences are the foundation of feeling good about ourselves and life.

My mother was the person who helped me understand and choose to take hurtful experiences as part of growing up. She enabled me and my two brothers, David and Michael, to make mistakes and grow, always helping us to see a valuable lesson in our actions.

Mom helped us get our feet in the water. It was our job to jump in and swim. She tried to surround us with positive influences and people. She always had that innate, intuitive understanding of what made us tick and how to help us on our journey. Today she's the first to say we haven't changed since our kindergarten days. How we were shaped in those early years still has an impact on our actions and passions today.

# Dr. Seuss

What you don't learn in kindergarten you can learn from Dr. Seuss. His books are great for kids of all ages. One of the best  is *Oh, the Places You'll Go!* Everything you need to be successful in life is in this book. Attitude, aptitude, and action are the theme.

> *"You have brains in your head.*
> *You have feet in your shoes.*
> *You can steer yourself*
> *Any direction you choose."*
> – Dr. Seuss

Dr. Seuss brings out the childlike wonder in us regardless of our age, helping us appreciate that we are always on wonderful journeys. These journeys start with the trials and tribulations of our early lives. As they continue, it's what we learned early in our life that determines what we get and where we go.

# Listening Skills

One of the first things we learn in kindergarten is how to listen. We are taught to raise our hand politely if we have something to say, and we are discouraged from interrupting others while they are speaking.

> *"The most important thing in communication*
> *is to hear what isn't being said."*
> – Peter Drucker

Just as you did in kindergarten, listen to others so you can understand their point of view. This is the foundation of empathy, which in turn is the key to great communication and understanding. Using empathy and understanding is very powerful. You should always hear someone's point of view before deciding to respond. When you hear the person's story, you get a better feeling for who they are and their perception of the particular situation. There may be a very good reason why they are acting or behaving a certain way. Don't judge until you hear what they're saying.

# Hearing vs. Listening

My son, Geoffrey, often says, "I hear you, but I'm not listening." This favorite expression of his sums up the way a lot of people handle communication. Others say they have selective hearing. There is an art to listening; it evolves around interest, curiosity, and focus.

You have two ears and one mouth. When meeting with someone, ask good questions and spend most of your time listening. Use the ears and mouth proportionately. Listen twice as much as you talk.

> **You can't learn much when your lips are moving.**

Do you remember show-and-tell in kindergarten? When it was your turn, you were thrilled to be the center of attention, to have everyone's eyes and ears trained on you. That human need and delight does not stop when you head into the next grade.

All through their lives, people appreciate it when you sit and listen to them. Listening is a very important ingredient in showing you care. The good listeners are the go-to people in friendships, relationships, families, and business. These people earn reputations as being wise and thoughtful – and it's all because of their ability to listen.

# KNOWLEDGE IS POWER

*"What makes Superman a hero is not that he has power,*
*but that he has the wisdom and maturity to use the power wisely."*
– Christopher Reeves

People take note of us if we have a good attitude, and they keep taking note of us if they see we have aptitude.

Sharing knowledge is good. Applying knowledge is even better. The core principle is to gain knowledge and interpret it though your senses and then take your belief or interpretation and apply it. Otherwise, what's the use of that knowledge?

Once you have knowledge, no one can ever take it away. However, application is key. Too many people know a lot and don't do anything with it. Power is the ability to act. Action takes knowledge and helps you gain success. Knowledge is who, what, when, how, why, and where. You must have knowledge to be effective and gain success.

## A Position of Strength

Knowledge is a position of strength. You can't really defeat it. You must get the facts because proof equals credibility. Do your homework and get the information. Develop the right skills. Gain the experience and gain knowledge. You can never have too much knowledge or too much information. With your knowledge, make things happen the way you want them to. Find good teachers and mentors to encourage the growth of your knowledge.

*"If you think education is expensive, try ignorance."*
– Derek Bok

The opposite of knowledge is ignorance. "Ignorance is bliss" just isn't true. What you don't know *will* hurt you. Misinformation is worse than ignorance; it can be very damaging. Just as knowledge is power, the lack of knowledge or reliance on misinformation is crippling, misleading, and harmful.

## *Circle of Knowledge*

There is a circle of knowledge made up of thirds. They are:

1. Unconsciously incompetent  (You don't know you don't know)
2. Consciously incompetent  (You know you don't know)
3. Consciously competent  (You know)

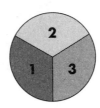

You want to move from 1 to 2 to 3. In so many areas of our lives, and as we grow and develop, we start in the first area. The power of aptitude is to get to 3.

Going through the stages of knowledge and competency is required no matter what we learn.

# BURDEN OF PROOF

If you are accused of something in a courtroom, it doesn't matter that you are innocent until proven guilty. You still need witnesses to speak on your behalf, against the prosecution's accusations. When one witness speaks up for you, your credibility spikes up. When another witness does so, it moves up exponentially. With three or four, you're on your way!

## Incredibly Credible

It doesn't matter what you do in life, whether professionally or personally. Your credibility is always on the line. Unless you can prove what you are stating is true, and unless others will step up to vouch for you, you could be in big trouble.

The proof of your credibility is what you are able to offer.

Aptitude and credibility are closely allied. People respect people with obvious skills and intelligence. If they should receive confirmation of your skills from hearing third-party testimonials, you will gain credibility in their eyes. People will buy into you more if they hear about you from someone else. If several people speak well of you, more people are likely to believe in you. It gets even better when you receive different types of "impersonal" support, such as mentions in newspapers and magazines or on the Internet.

People love numbers. If your testimonial contains numbers depicting your effect on market share or diagrams showing your upward movement or achievements, they will respond favorably.

## Proof and Credibility

Lots of proof equals lots of credibility, proof to prove the proof. The more proof you have, the more convincing and credible you become. This is not meant to overwhelm people but to help substantiate your efforts when you're attempting to reach agreement or make a statement. With this proof, you are able to show "beyond a shadow of a doubt" that your position is right.

## Testimonials

### Personal testimonials

Testimonials from people you know, in written form, give you proof and credibility when you're looking for a job. Nothing works better and adds more value than praise from your peers and internal customers. It's important to get these proof statements/references from your boss or an executive, which adds even more credibility. Additionally, letters from your external customers validate what you're trying to prove to your prospective employer.

You can ask colleagues, superiors, and peers to write these letters, but it is rare that they will. The numbers say only approximately 10% of people will actually comply – writing letters is too time-consuming.

Write your own testimonials and ask your references to sign them. By writing them yourself, you can highlight, outline, and focus on your strengths. You must then ask the person who is signing them if they have anything to add or delete. You can also email the testimonial and ask them to add or delete what they want.

### Business testimonials

Hang on to testimonials from pleased customers praising your company and you. Always follow up on these. Update your file by seeking for more recent feedback.

Testimonials can be verbal. You may ask a customer or person on a regular basis to provide verbal testimonials/references. You can have a prospective customer or employer call them. It's critical that you let them know that they're going to be called and what you would like them to relay.

It's proper etiquette to first ask people whether they mind being called, because circumstances are always changing. Keep people informed as to why you are using them. Get permission each and every time you use them. People don't mind helping you out in this way as long as you are polite enough to apprise them of what's happening.

The more testimonials, the greater the credibility for you, especially when it comes to business testimonials. Another option is to take snippets from testimonials and put pages of anonymous quotes together. This is less personal but still drives the point home.

When I was in my first sales job, I put together a book filled with testimonials from happy customers saying why they did business with us. This was very useful for us because we weren't as well known, established, or big as our competitors. The fact that I had a large number of testimonials made a huge difference. It made people more comfortable in deciding to do business with us.

Good testimonials help you establish and maintain a strong personal brand. Whether you're using a testimonial, recommendation, or referral, promote yourself – in the end, you are your own best testimonial.

## *Earning the Right*

An expression that I have heard for years is that someone has "earned the right." It is spoken of a person who has taken the time to build a relationship with someone or a company and has "deposited" enough time and value to get something in return.

In other words, you pay the price of time and learning, to be reciprocated later in life. Pablo Picasso was once asked how he could possibly charge thousands of dollars for sketches that took him only a few minutes to complete. His answer: "It took me a lifetime to create these sketches." The great artist had paid the price and learned his skill over years of trial and error. He had earned the right to charge that amount.

Sometimes when we hire someone to do something we cannot do, we begrudge them their fee. We feel they are taking advantage of us. However, we are not paying for just this one individual expression of their skill. We are paying for the time, experience, and expertise they have put in to perfect their skills, talents, and capabilities.

# READ THE BOOKS

Back in the 1980s, I heard Jim Rohn speak in Toronto to an audience of 2,000 people. He spoke about success and shared his wisdom about a happy, fulfilling life. Rohn had a profound impact on me, changing my life in two key areas: writing and reading. He sparked an incredible passion in me that burns within me to this day. He talked about the power of keeping journals, which I immediately began to do.

*"The mind is like a parachute. It works best when it is open."*
— Albert Einstein

He also talked about why it was so important to read books. Prior to that moment, it just hadn't occurred to me how powerful and important books could be. Rohn's repetition of the phrase "read the books" in his southern drawl set something off in me that soon became a passionate fire. Since that day I have become an avid reader. And I do more than just read the books. I enjoy studying and rereading them.

## Read and Study

When I'm really enjoying a book, I read and reread it, highlighting areas and writing my own ideas in the margins. I then transfer the highlighted areas and my ideas into a journal. I also get the audio version of some of these books and listen to them again and again. Each time I listen, I gain more insight, retain more, and learn more.

What exactly do I write in the margins? Any ideas that arise as I am reading. Concepts spark an idea of how I believe I can help others. I add my own knowledge and experiences to build on the foundations of what catches my attention. I write down what is worth passing on to others. In this way I tap into the experiences of others and filter their experiences and wisdom in order to transfer knowledge to others. My interpretations, combined with those of others, help fuel my imagination.

## *Books for Your Life Library*

Here are just a few of the books that make up the foundation of my life library. These are the ones I go back to again and again. My library is one of my most prized possessions. It is something that I feel will be a great asset to pass on to my kids.

- *Think and Grow Rich*, Napoleon Hill. A great philosophy for motivational life success.
- *Dig Your Well Before You're Thirsty*, Harvey Mackay. Networking concepts... how to connect with people.
- *The Power of Focus*, Jack Canfield, Mark Victor Hansen, Les Hewitt. Goals and strategies for success.
- *Good to Great*, Jim Collins. An excellent business book ... how to succeed in Biz and Life.
- *The Seven Habits of Highly Effective People*, Stephen R. Covey. Creating great habits for life.
- *Who Moved My Cheese?* Spencer Johnson, M.D. Getting comfortable with change.
- *Fish!* Stephen Lundin, Harry Paul, John Christensen. It's all about attitude.
- *Don't Sweat the Small Stuff*, Richard Carlson. Life lessons and anecdotes.
- *Body for Life*, Bill Phillips. Great for health and fitness.
- *Rich Dad Poor Dad*, Robert Kiyosaki. Wealth strategies and finance.
- *Success Is a Choice*, Rick Pitino. Learn and thrive on success.
- *The Precious Present*, Spencer Johnson, M.D. Be in the present moment.
- *The Alchemist*, Paul Coelho. Life lessons.
- *It's Not About the Bike*, Lance Armstrong. The power of determination and persistence.
- *We Got Fired! ... And It's the Best Thing That Ever Happened to Us*, Harvey Mackay. Learn from change.
- *Oh, the Places You'll Go!* Dr. Seuss. Life lessons for kids of all ages.
- *Bulls, Bears and Pigs*, David Cork (my brother). Balance in your financial life.
- *How to Win Friends and Influence People*, Dale Carnegie. Just like the title says ...

# JUICE YOUR SENSES

The average person tends to retain anywhere from 10% to 15% of what they hear or see. Repetition helps us retain more – sometimes each repetition gains us 10% or more. There is a lot of truth to the saying "repetition is the mother of skill." This may sound excessive, but if you truly want to retain information – if you want to reinforce what you already know, and feel good about what you know – repetition is a must.

One thing that helps us get to 75% to 90% retention is juicing our senses. Seeing or hearing or even acting out the same or similar message five or six times increases retention rates dramatically.

## Juice Your Reading

Try the following steps when you read a book. Highlight what you like and write in the margins. You can add your own interpretations or thoughts of what you have just read as you are reading it and the ideas are flowing. This will help you to go back and then add what you think is important or helpful. In your quest to learn, you should write your thoughts down, not just in the margins of a book, but also in a journal.

Tap into your sense of hearing by getting the book in an audio version.

By using sight, touch, and hearing, you have juiced three of five senses. In this way, you will become an expert, truly gaining greater knowledge.

Not only do your senses get a workout, so do the Three A's. By rereading, you are enhancing your aptitude and what you learn will influence your attitude. By repeating your reading, watching, or listening, you are acting on what you have learned.

Always be aware that the more senses you can use the better. The goal is to juice all five, if possible, in all that you do. In the Straight-A's world, all the A's are driven by your senses and the knowledge that comes as you involve and use them again and again.

## *The Real Wonders of the World*

Here's a great story that I ran across recently.

A group of students were asked to list what they thought were the Seven Wonders of the World. Though there were some disagreements among them, the following received the most votes:

1. Egypt's Great Pyramids
2. Taj Mahal, India
3. Grand Canyon, Arizona
4. Panama Canal
5. Empire State Building, New York
6. St. Peter's Basilica, Rome
7. China's Great Wall

While gathering the votes, the teacher noticed that one student had not finished her list. So she asked the girl if she was having trouble.

"Yes, a little," the girl replied. "I couldn't quite make up my mind because there were so many."

"Well, tell us what you have, and maybe we can help," the teacher said.

The girl hesitated, then read to the class her Seven Wonders of the World:

1. To see
2. To hear
3. To touch
4. To taste
5. To feel
6. To laugh
   ...and
7. To love

The things we overlook as simple and ordinary are truly wondrous. We need a gentle reminder that the most precious things in life cannot be bought or created but are ours to begin with.

# PUT IT IN WRITING

Journals are an excellent means of retaining knowledge. All my experiences and learning go into the ones I keep. I started my first journal eighteen years ago and begin a new one every six months. I can track my perspective on events, books, ideas, jokes by going back and rereading them, which I do often. When I look back in this way, I see what I was doing and what was important to me at the time.

In fact, I have mined my journals for nuggets and ideas in putting this book together.

## Doing Inventory

The great thing about journals is how they help you use your past to chart your future. They bring awareness and can help you avoid repeating mistakes. A journal is like an inventory of your assets, strengths, experiences, achievements, and hopes. It can be a projection of what is going to happen in your life.

When you keep a journal, you quickly see the value of its being for your eyes only. No one's going to judge you for what you've written. If you want to share your journal, that is your choice.

Your journal should include your goals, greatest successes, and any educational or training programs attended and what you picked up from them. You can have all sorts of lists to refer back to, or share with mentors, influencers, or role models. Your journal may include processes, stories of inspiration, people who touched and inspired you, and quotes that have sparked insight.

## My Favorite Journal

I have talked about journal writing with my children for years. When my daughter, Stephanie, was sixteen, she had a wonderful opportunity to go to school in

France for six weeks, living with a French family outside Paris. Before she left, I gave her a journal for capturing her feelings and experiences while there. Before I gave it to her, I wrote my 50 favorite quotes in it, one at the top of each of the first 50 pages. I asked her to write down her interpretation of what each quote meant. Teenager that she was, her response was, "I'll fill it in if I get bored."

I figured my chances of getting her to write anything were maybe, at best, 50%.

When my daughter returned from her excursion, she handed me a full journal. Each and every page had at least a dozen points written on it.

"I got bored. I had nothing better to do," she told me.

I was very excited to read her journal. It was absolutely astonishing. So much wisdom came through in her words.

This journal proved to me that my kids were listening to me a lot more than they liked to admit. I'd been feeding them with the power of books and audio tapes since birth. Having my daughter's journal among my own is simply priceless to me.

Kids are never too young to start this wonderful habit.

## *Releasing the Flow*

> *"I Keep six honest serving-men:*
> *(They taught me all I know);*
> *Their names are What and Why and When*
> *And How and Where and Who."*
> – *Rudyard Kipling*

Whenever I am planning, setting goals, and networking, which are the foundational parts of my blueprint for life, I always think things through by writing down as many answers as possible to each of these six questions. These words are always part of the strategy for getting Straight A's in life. They will keep you on course. They will help you balance health, family, self-improvement, and career.

It's amazing how these "servants" assist me when I'm stuck. Just asking what I want to accomplish, why that will help me or others, when the best time is to implement it, how I will implement it, and so on, releases a wonderful flow of ideas and possibilities.

# IT TAKES A TEAM

Edison didn't know every scientific concept and principle. But he had the wisdom to surround himself with those who together knew much more than he did. These smart people were his "mastermind" group. Each of these people had a profound effect on his life and work.

This is characteristic of great people. One of the chief signs of their aptitude is how they tap into the knowledge of others. They know there is power in numbers, groups, and teams.

## Mastermind Groups

You can build your own mastermind group. You may also be called on to join such a group. These groups:

- Need to meet regularly
- Should have members with diverse backgrounds
- Should be composed of people who have overcome challenges and are successful in the business world
- Take a commitment from every member
- Maintain confidentiality, integrity, and trust

## What to Discuss

- The best thing that has happened since the last meeting
- What's happening in members' business lives
- What's happening in their personal lives
- Great challenges

- Opportunities through networking
- Goals to go after

Brilliant people do brilliant work. Getting to know people with lots of aptitude is an important step on the way to your prosperity, whether emotional or financial. Confidence is a habit that can be honed and strengthened.

Our untapped potential can be a frightening thing. People are ridiculously powerful when they set their minds on a single task. A mastermind group can take that to the next level. Your group could also be a book club. You could share the knowledge you've gained from a book you're reading together, taking this knowledge to the next level in your thinking and learning.

## Mentors

When it comes to developing your aptitude, it is important to find a mentor and act as a mentor to someone else. A good mentor is someone who can help you grow by transferring their wisdom and experience to you. These are people I refer to as the eagles, the people who help you fly to new heights.

A mentor can even be someone whose books you have read. Authors are more approachable than you may think. In fact, a lot of them love to leave their computer screens from time to time and interact with "live readers." However, even if you can't meet them, you can dip into their books and let them teach you.

I have a number of these types of mentors. Some of them have had a profound impact on my life. One is Jim Rohn, the motivational speaker I referred to above. I don't meet with him, but his effect on me is ongoing. The same is true of Brian Tracey, Lance Armstrong, and Oprah. They don't know that they are my mentors, but they have made many contributions to my life and learning.

Your mentors can come in all shapes and sizes and know you or not, but they are the select few who impact you and help you on your journey to success. They are the ones who help you define the Straight A's you are striving toward.

### *Collaboration Is Part of Success*

The Nobel Prize winner John Forbes Nash, mentioned earlier in this book, built his success by traveling down already existing mathematical paths while searching for his own advances until he finally achieved success. We often forget this about geniuses. They are not geniuses because they come up with something out of the blue that no one else has ever thought of. They are geniuses because they build on the proven foundations of the geniuses who have gone before them.

Geniuses may be anti-social, but their successes are nevertheless collaborative in nature. They are socializing in their minds and hearts with the greats preceding them, even if their competitive fires are pushing them to do something different or better than these creative forebears.

The same is true for most of us. We may not be geniuses, but we move ahead in developing our aptitude by understanding basic concepts and then pushing the limits to explore uncharted waters.

Great successes are collaborative in nature, built on previous learning tapped from experts. We build our own successes on the foundational principles, concepts, and strategies of others.

# MY THREE WISE MEN

> *"The next best thing to being wise oneself*
> *is to live in a circle of those who are."*
> – *C.S. Lewis*

I have been blessed in my life and career by having three wise men to turn to for advice and support. It's in the nature of wise men to bear gifts, and these three, respectively, have given me the gifts of partnership, coaching, and mentoring.

## Wise Man #1

John was a great business partner I was fortunate to work with in the 1980s. He held me accountable for reaching my goals, and I did the same for him. This was so important to us early in our professional lives. We were both in sales in an organization that was a rocket heading straight for the stars.

The feature of our relationship was a little routine we followed.

John and I would call each other every morning to see what the other was doing and to kick-start the day. One way or the other, and very informally, we asked each other what our goals were for that day, how we were going to achieve them, and how they fit into our longer-term objectives. Two elements of this routine combined powerfully for us: the expectation of honesty and the assurance of positive support, no matter what.

Through this routine we could catch each other on any tendency to waver in our resolve. We could also sniff out any inconsistency in the way we were going about our business. Furthermore, the personal and professional merged in a unique way. As we went through life together, our family challenges and joys, our personal blocks to growth, any tendencies to shy away from business challenges – all these were fair game for the probing questions we asked each other.

## Wise Man #2

Ted was the first person to have faith in my abilities, giving me my first management job. He believed in me and instilled confidence in me. By giving me responsibility and then continuously coaching and mentoring me, he helped me feel good about my abilities and learn how to manage people.

Of my three wise men, Ted has been a consistent, continuous teacher, helping to reinforce what I already knew and came to know about the art of management. What was so special about his wisdom was seeing him living out, day by day, what he was teaching me. He was managing me in exactly the way he taught me to manage others. Powerful!

Ted, who has been a coach, mentor, and friend for the past sixteen years, is my go-to guy when I need advice, ideas, and support.

## Wise Man #3

The third and most recent wise man is Raymond. Through his teaching and mentorship, I have gained confidence in my current work in career coaching and motivational speaking.

Like me, Raymond is a motivator and teacher. Where my other wise men helped me primarily in the practice of my profession, he has taught me a great deal about setting and achieving goals and the law of attraction.

Raymond's wisdom has helped me have confidence that I will achieve my goals through practicing simple, consistent disciplines each and every day.

Raymond helps me by pulling out of me and reinforcing what I already know. Often he steps outside the teaching role and simply helps me feel good about my accomplishments and direction in life.

I am grateful to my three wise men and continue to look for others to help me in my continual thirst to reach excellence in all areas of my life.

# BE THE TEACHER

Stephen Covey, in his book *The 8th Habit*, talks about the power of teaching. He even suggests having your kids teach you their schoolwork so they have to learn it by teaching it. Such a simple idea ... why didn't someone think of this before?

A critical ingredient in developing your aptitude, then, is to be the teacher in your approach to learning. When you teach, you see things more clearly and retain more.

Why? Because when you have to teach something you spend more time learning it. I have even found myself saying things on the fly during a speech that I hadn't planned for that presentation – things that fall into place because of the combination of preparing my speech and then seeking to get my thoughts across to the people in front of me.

Teaching also heightens your confidence as you learn to hold the attention of groups, whether formal or informal, on a topic.

## Teaching Is Doing

From the very moment you know you are going to teach, your learning is affected. You pay more attention to what you're doing because you're mentally filing away explanations and examples. Earlier in the book I advised you to be a host not a guest. Similarly, be the teacher, not a student.

The great thing about this is that it will make you a better student.

*"To teach is to learn twice."*
– Joseph Joubert

Most of us forget what we've learned within the last 48 hours. By teaching, you retain information longer and better. Teach your children and get them to teach you. This is an excellent way to improve their grades, because to teach you, they must learn at a much deeper level.

### *Three Activities That Build on Each Other*

1. Learning
2. Teaching
3. Doing

# MANAGE THOSE PERCEPTIONS

> *"What is a weed? A plant whose virtues
> have not yet been discovered."*
> – Ralph Waldo Emerson

You know what an apple tastes like, but if you asked ten different people how one tastes, odds are you will get ten very different answers.

People with aptitude understand that people sometimes see things very differently. Differences in perception come into play in all of human behavior. Our perception is our reality.

## Perceptions, Perceptions

**Is a zebra black with white stripes, or white with black stripes?**

Things do not always happen the way we remember, but the way we remember is how they happened in our perception. Perceptions are our interpretation of how things happened. They are the result of things being filtered through the knowledge we have learned through experience. So reality is not necessarily what actually happened but the way we, or others, say it happened.

Answers aren't always black and white. There will be many gray areas in your personal and business life. Perception is your reality, or another person's reality. Without clear perceptions, you will be clouded by uncertainty.

Because of the reality of perception, if something is important to you in your dealings with people, you should meet them face to face to discuss it. You may feel that someone else will express your message better or more eloquently than you, and that it will be passed on as you have asked. But entrusting them with your message may be a huge risk. Even if you put it in writing, it may change from your initial intention. The moment your message is filtered through someone else, it will take on another perception or interpretation.

And don't forget the power of body language, presence, and making a good impression. You may have a lot more impact if you make the effort yourself, personally. Don't leave the situation to someone else who may not care as much as you do.

For example, when job hunting, it is important to go in person. If you look good, dress well, and have good body language, you will have an edge as you get in front of decision makers.

## Broken Telephone

Phil Collins reminds us, in his song "Both Sides of the Story," that we should always get the other side of the story, and this is true both inside and outside the business world. Too often we hear a story and make a quick judgment. We, and our actions, are shaped by that first impression. We're not likely to change our initial reaction, but we can at least listen to the other side of the story. Weighing the facts before making a decision is still the best way.

To see how important this is, play a game of broken telephone. Get a group of people to sit in a circle and have someone whisper a short story to the person next to them. Then have that person tell the person next to them. Proceed in this way around the circle. Have the final person then tell the story based on what they heard and the first person repeat the original story. You will be amazed by how the story has changed!

It just proves how differently people interpret what they hear.

### *From No to Know*

Change your perception of the word "no."

No is not necessarily the final word. It does not have to be a devastating personal rejection. It can mean anything you want it to mean.

> **"No" and "know" are both part of the word "knowledge."**

When you hear a no you must analyze the situation and decide if an opportunity lies behind these two little letters.

Lack of knowledge is what makes people translate a no into a rejection. The presence of know helps you understand what to do when you've come up against a negative.

So, qualify the no. Never accept it at face value. Imagine the no you hear as a question. See it as a challenge. No really means "Can you be more creative? Can you do better than that?"

# THINK OUTSIDE
# THE BOX

*"Thinking is easy, acting is difficult, and to put one's thoughts into action is the most difficult thing in the world."*
*– Goethe*

1. Draw three rows of three dots
2. Then, using only four lines, and without lifting your pencil, connect the dots

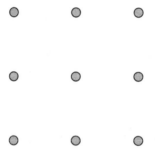

*Solution:* You must put the lines outside the box to complete the task. Most people will try to keep the lines within the parameters of the box, even though the directions did not specify that they should do so.

This little exercise simulates how people think on a regular basis. They try to remain within their comfort zone, or "inside the box," failing to break the rules or go beyond the expected boundaries.

Now try this one:

1. Draw an X on the page
2. Now change that X into the number 6

*Solution:* Many will say this is impossible because X consists of two straight lines whereas the number 6 consists of a circle and a curved line. However, you can create the # sign by adding lines to the X and then write the number 6 beside it, or add the letters SI before the X, spelling out the word SIX.

I believe my concept that you should give, give, give in networking is outside the traditional box. People in need of a job or new opportunity think they should network in order to get, get, get. But my point is that when your attitude is in give mode rather than get mode, you will release the true power of networking.

This is definitely outside the box. A large number of the speakers I've heard at networking events and other large gatherings ask people in the audience to find another person and introduce themselves. The two people spend a few minutes exchanging niceties and getting to know each other to see if there is some connection that could help them in their job search. This exercise focuses on what's in it for me. I always get the audience to go deeper and think about what they can do for the other person. This puts the give attitude in motion.

# THE GIFT OF THE PRESENT

> *"Yesterday is history. Tomorrow is a mystery. And today?*
> *Today is a gift. That's why we call it the present."*
> — *Babatunde Olatunji*

You learn from the past. It represents your experience and is something you can't change.

It is said that there is no such thing as failure. You can chalk up anything you experience to learning. Failure is an opportunity to learn how not to do something the next time. You can learn from it and get on with your life.

The future is something you plan for, dream toward, and envision. You can't control the future; you can only plan toward it. The more you plan and focus, the greater the probability that it will look like your vision. Of course, when uncontrollable events occur, your plan may need to be adjusted.

## Open the Present

The only area you can truly control is the present. You are always in the present. You are your present attitude, aptitude, and action. The Three A's are most powerful in the present.

Ask yourself if what you did yesterday to get yourself where you are today is enough to get you where you want to be tomorrow.

Your experience today is the result of your past choices and your choices today will be your experiences of tomorrow. Every experience yesterday, today, and tomorrow is the result of how you respond to events in your life. Carpe diem – seize the day! Live the moment. You have power over your present. Be present – be there at the moment and in the moment. Open all your senses to the present. Listen, observe, smell, speak, taste, and touch. Juice the senses.

## The Greatest Gift

Be present for the people around you. The greatest gift to anyone is to listen to them and show you care, whether you're in a conversation at work or with family or friends. This is what being in the present means in its truest form.

As Linden Wood put it, "People don't care how much you know until they know how much you care." Or as I always put it, **you have to know to care and care to know**. Caring is being present. When you are in the present it helps others enjoy the present and share the moment. Why do we love photos? Because they capture the present forever, allowing us to enjoy reliving the moment.

*"Today is the tomorrow we worried about yesterday."*
— *Anonymous*

Once gone, the present will never return, but in reality we are always in the present. Fully present means fully focused and engaged. When you show genuine enthusiasm, focus, and attention to a customer, family member, or friend it enriches the moment. You have to have an external focus on them, rather than an internal focus on yourself, to help the other person relish the present with you.

## How Good Does It Get?

Spending time with your kids or loved ones is as good as it gets. Savor and enjoy the moment. People are always thinking about how things will get better. Instead, enjoy the here and now.

Be thankful for the present and how you are able to share it with other special people in your life. Live life to the fullest. Absorb and don't regret.

A father and teenage daughter sit on a beach in Hawaii as the sun goes down. The temperature is perfect. The view of the beach and the ocean are perfect. But the dad is clearly worried that he is not making life come out perfectly for his daughter.

"Dad," she says, "this is as good as it gets. This may be the best moment of your life. How much better do you want it?"

Like all children, she wants him to savor the present moment with her.

*"Learn how to be happy with what you have while you*
*pursue all that you want."*
— *Jim Rohn*

What one person enjoys, another may despise. One person's junk is another person's treasure. Enjoyment comes from your attitude in a particular situation, not just the situation itself. Stop searching for and start enjoying. Forget the coulda, woulda, shoulda. As they say, don't should all over yourself. Moments make your life ... when you realize them, your life will never be quite the same.

PART THREE

# ACTION

| | |
|---|---|
| Habits | Ask |
| Networking | Disciplines |
| Goals | 80/20 Rule |
| Give (G7) | Eagles |
| Time | Affirmations |
| Scoreboard | Edison |
| Fundamentals | Terry & Rick |
| Determination | Personal Contract |
| Execution | Map/Blueprint |

# YOUR SUCCESS STORY

> *"Luck is what happens when preparation meets opportunity."*
> — *Seneca*

Action is the third and final A in the Straight-A's formula for life. We can now build on our foundation of attitude and aptitude. We can now act in accordance with these so that success becomes second nature to us – a habit of behaving in successful ways.

A good place to begin our journey together on the topic of the third A, action, is to look at our past actions – specifically, our past successes.

Knowing your greatest successes is the foundation of your continuing success. These successes are defining moments in your life that have left a powerful mark on the way you see yourself.

## Think Back as Far as Your Memory Takes You

- What are your greatest successes to date?
- What achievements are you proudest of?
- Think about successes in sports, health, family, self-improvement, academics, charity, helping someone. Balance is critical in developing your list.

## Your Greatest Successes to Date

Write down a list in point form of the greatest successes in your life to date. Dr. Phil would call these your defining moments. When you have completed it, your list should include ten to fifteen items. Following is a chart to use in completing this exercise.

A theme or themes will emerge as you look at your list. If you're like most people, you will see a pattern, and that pattern is you.

Maybe you were on sports teams and that's the theme, or you were a good student and that keeps showing up. This list reveals your passions through life and what has made a difference and motivated you.

# MY GREATEST SUCCESSES TO DATE

## (What I am proudest of)

1.

2.

3.

4.

5.

6.

7.

8.

9.

10.

11.

12.

13.

14.

15.

16.

17.

18.

19.

20.

This also is a feel-good list. Too often we spend time thinking about things that didn't happen rather than reflecting on all the amazing things that have – our accomplishments and the great contributions we've made.

Keep this list and add to it as you achieve more successes or as you remember ones you forgot to put down. Whenever you're having a bad day or feeling down on yourself, pull out this list and look at all your accomplishments. You've done some pretty great things. Celebrate them!

## Review to Renew

This list serves to give us that pat on the back that we don't give ourselves often enough. Review your list often. It will highlight your natural abilities and show that you've developed some excellent habits. These are the most powerful habits, the ones that will lead to continuing success.

Here are some examples, including a few of my own:

- My kids
- My marriage
- Being there for my mother as she conquered cancer
- Working with a children's charity
- My Best Athlete award in grade six
- Graduating from university
- Helping a brother through a difficult time
- Playing professional hockey in Europe
- My first job
- My first big paycheck
- My hole-in-one at the golf club
- My daughter graduating from university
- My trip to the Great Wall in China
- The presentation I did in front of the company
- The major project I finished
- The bonus I got for _____
- The first year I made over $50,000 or $150,000
- Losing 50 pounds, and keeping them off
- Running a marathon
- Meeting Oprah

My list is eleven years old and I add to it continually. I now have 37 items, including greatest successes, defining moments, things that make me proud, and my strengths, passions, and loves. I look at it all the time to remind me that I have accomplished some amazing goals. I put this list into every new journal I write so it is always front and center for me.

Marcus Buckingham and Donald Clifton, in their bestselling book *Now, Discover Your Strengths*, talk about building on your strengths and focusing on what you do well. What you do well is generally what you love. You must spend more time on what you do well and what motivates you. You are more productive when working from your strengths. These tend to be your natural abilities and will always attract your interest.

> *"Unfortunately, most of us have little sense of our talents and strengths, much less the ability to build our lives around them. Instead, guided by our parents, by our teachers, by our managers, and by psychology's fascination with pathology, we become experts in our weaknesses and spend our lives trying to repair these flaws, while our strengths lie dormant and neglected."*
> – *Marcus Buckingham*

Are you doing this with your kids? When they bring home their report cards, do you focus on where they are excelling? When you see an A in English, an A in History, a B in Geography, a B in Physical Education, and then a D or E in Biology, which grades capture your attention?

We tend to spend most of our time working with our kids on their weak subjects. But is that where we should be concentrating our efforts? When they do well in a subject, it's because of a combination of natural strength and enjoyment. Perhaps we should help them more in these areas.

## *A Look Back*

Studies say we don't change that much from when we were young. When you bump into people on the street or meet them at a high-school reunion and you haven't seen them in 20 or 30 years, have they changed? Not that much. Their attitudes are still the same. They have learned a lot more and have experienced a great deal more, but for the most part their basic aptitude is still the same. Whether they have found a way to leverage their attitudes and aptitudes into a successful career and family life is a whole other question.

**Success is built on success. Once you have the foundation ... keep building.**

The Three A's exist early on in our lives and stay with us for most of it. They revolve on our passions and our vision of how we want to live. Studies say that what we are driven by and passionate about were apparent in us at a very young age.

And beyond what the content of our passions and drives may be, we tend to approach life a certain way – and have approached life this way since our earliest days. Our approach is the DNA of our behavior. If we can pursue what makes us feel good and incorporate it into our working lives, we will have found something we love to do and it won't really be work. Follow that passion of what really makes you happy. Look back to your childhood and teenage years to see what you focused on or what was or is your greatest pleasure.

There's no doubt about it, our early dreams and aspirations are still with us. The exciting opportunity before us is to find them, and once we have, to build on them.

# FAILURE
## (A. K. A. EXPERIENCE)

> *"There are two kinds of failures: those who thought and never did,
> and those who did and never thought."*
> — Laurence J. Peter

| |
|---|
| **Failure is a prerequisite for success.** |

On the other side of the coin of success is failure. Everything you do in life on a day-to-day basis puts you face to face with failure and rejection. As Jim Rohn says, "What's easy to do – is easy not to do." The key is to deal with failure positively and not take it personally. You must jump in, experience, and keep moving forward.

## Goals, Failure, and Character

We avoid setting goals because we fear rejection. That makes sense, because when we set goals we are continually bombarded with negative feedback. "What a ridiculous idea ... that will never work" is an often-heard response to a new idea. Or "Why bother? No one can do what you're talking about." We begin to believe what we hear, which can send us spiraling into self-doubt and paralysis.

The other main reason people don't even set goals is a fear of failure. This is the biggest obstacle to success in adult life. We allow a psychological wall to build up around us and our youthful aspirations. We become afraid to try new things, content to live in narrower and narrower confines. It's as if we put ourselves on house arrest.

> *"Every human being is driven by their need to avoid pain or their
> desire to gain pleasure. Procrastination is the silent killer."*
> — Tony Robbins

People don't understand the importance of failure in achievement. Failure is a prerequisite to success. It is a part of the learning process. We must be willing to look openly into our failures and build on them. We must fall on our faces, get up, dust ourselves off, and feel good about the lessons learned. This will help us gain the strength to move on to the next level. Everybody falls from time to time. The true winners are the ones who get back up immediately, learn from their experiences, and strive to be better.

It's what you learn in the process of trying to achieve goals that molds and makes you what you are. Character is formed when you fail to meet a goal and learn from that failure. It is formed when you accept the truth about why things didn't go the way you anticipated. Not only does this strengthen your attitude in response to failure, it also serves to minimize the number of failures you experience.

> **There is no such thing as failure, only experience.**

When you're not afraid of failure, you're not afraid of challenges. Being open to challenges is what will keep you young and flexible. Challenges are what make life so much fun.

Perhaps the key point about failure is that you must accept yourself regardless of what happens. That is the attitude of success.

## A "Colonel" of Truth

Colonel Harlan Sanders was broke and 65 years old when his first social security check came in – for $102. He knew he had to get back to work, and he knew he had only one salable asset: a chicken recipe. So he traveled America trying to license the use of his recipe. Some nights he slept in his car. But his persistence and determination to keep going no matter how often he was rejected helped him succeed beyond what most people could ever dream.

Despite thousands of rejections, his efforts eventually took off, creating the Kentucky Fried Chicken empire and making him one of the most recognizable people in advertising history. Everyone knows the Colonel.

# FAILURE = SUCCESS

> *"Failure is the opportunity to begin again more intelligently."*
> *— Henry Ford*

Thomas Watson, the founder of IBM, came up with a great concept. He said that in order to double your success, you must double your failure. Failure is part of the process and the journey. The higher we travel up the success ladder, the more failure we will encounter. When we understand this concept and live by it, the sky's the limit.

In other words, bring it on.

## Embrace Failure

Life is not always rainbows and butterflies. You must take the risks and get out of your comfort zone. Thomas Edison is one of the greatest inventors of all time – and one of the biggest failures of all times. He failed thousands of times before creating the light bulb, and experimented 17,000 times with botanical specimens over a four-year period for another of his patents.

> *"Genius is 1% inspiration and 99% perspiration."*
> *— Thomas Edison*

Edison always followed two rules: first, starting with the end in mind, and second, believing it's not a matter of if, but when. His philosophy, when he set a goal, was to take action and do whatever it took to achieve that goal. The reason he is one of the greatest inventors who ever lived is that he never let the word "impossible" stop him.

In one famous interaction with the press, Edison was challenged regarding why he would make so many attempts in trying to create the light bulb. "Mr. Edison, you have failed over a thousand times in trying to create your light bulb," one reporter said.

"I have not failed but found a thousand ways in which it doesn't work, so I am a thousand steps closer to achieving my goals," Edison replied.

What a great philosophy for life!

## *The Price of Success*

There is no such thing as instant success. Every successful person is willing to pay a price and take action toward achieving success. They do whatever it takes.

In his book *Good to Great*, Jim Collins talks about the giant flywheel and how it takes push after push to get it moving. In fact, the flywheel doesn't start moving until after thousands of pushes. Is it the first push, the 100th push, or the 1000th push that makes it move? None of the above. it is the accumulation of pushes. Whether in business or your personal life, it is a sustained effort, push by push, that will make the difference.

They say it takes years to become an overnight success. Shania Twain spent years of hard work, dedication, determination, persistence, and patience before everything gelled and she became an international superstar. Very few people get to where they are on the ladder of success without paying the price of hard work. It's a process of living and learning through the Straight A's and continually taking action in the direction of your goals.

For example, in health and fitness it's repetition, day after day, that makes the difference. When I tell people I do 200 crunches every morning, it doesn't seem like a lot. But when you add it up over a year, it's a huge number – over 73,000 crunches. The sustained effort every day is what makes the difference and keeps me in good shape.

# YOUR RECIPE FOR SUCCESS

*My list of ingredients for success is divided into four basic groups.*
*Inward. Outward. Upward. And Onward.*
— David Thomas

New ingredients can improve any recipe – including your recipe for success.

Most of the time, both consciously and subconsciously, we borrow ingredients. We create our recipes from what we hear and see – after all, very few things these days are original.

## Our Unique Ingredients

But we are all unique and can make use of these ingredients in unique ways. We are always evolving. Depending on our present circumstances and the ingredients we create, choose, and borrow, we may come up with a success that's totally different from other people's.

The three essential ingredients of anyone's recipe for success are the Straight A's of attitude, aptitude, and action. You can't have one without the others.

What's your recipe for success?

Here's a great recipe for success in life that I came across recently:

- 3 cups love
- 2 cups loyalty
- 3 cups forgiveness
- 5 tablespoons hope
- 2 tablespoons tenderness
- 4 quarts sharing
- 2 barrels of laughter

Take the love and loyalty and mix it with sharing. Blend it with tenderness, forgiveness, and hope. Sprinkle abundantly with laughter. Bake it with sunshine. Serve daily in generous helpings.

The ingredients you put into life make a powerful statement about you. My favorite recipe is:

Start with a huge amount of attitude, created through a combination of dreaming, vision, passion, belief, desire, self-esteem, confidence, and body language. Add aptitude, which is created by a combination of knowledge, learning, education, study, intelligence, books, and CDs. Add action, which is created from a combination of planning, networking, goals, execution, determination, discipline, and polite persistence. Then add a pinch of failure, fear, rejection, and change. Sift until it becomes experience. Stir until it's ready to serve.

# MASTERMINDS OF SUCCESS

> *"If you hear a voice within you say 'you cannot paint,'
> then by all means paint, and that voice will be silenced."*
> – *Vincent van Gogh*

Everyone has a Jon Levy in their life. Someone who is a great example of how the Three A's can come together.

Jon is someone who gets Straight A's in everything he does. He worked hard to achieve success in business. He is the co-founder, with his brother, Andy, of the business Mastermind Educational. They are now reaping the fruits of 20 years of determination and persistence.

## A Passion for Success

They started out with a small store and worked for a few years out of the basement of Andy's house. They had a vision and they believed in what they were doing. Their attitudes and passion for success never wavered. They learned through their experiences, both good and bad, building their chain of successful specialty educational toy stores.

| If your mind can see it, you can achieve it. |
| --- |

They didn't supply a store that was in demand. They created demand for a certain kind of store. People wanted more than just educational toys, software, and books for their kids – they wanted an experience. Jon created this through his great attitude. He and his brother created great selection and prompt, excellent service. Is it any surprise that all of their employees demonstrate a wonderful attitude?

Jon is a giver. He personifies balance. He always asks what he can do for you and how he can help. Giving in life and business is his number-one priority and his number-one reason for success. He supports several charities, including a wonderful camp for learning-challenged children called Camp Kirk, run by Henri Audet. Jon has chaired the camp's drive to raise capital for these kids, putting in many hours to help make the project work.

For Jon it seems effortless. He doesn't question the why, he just knows it's the right thing to do and does it. Jon has the knowledge and the aptitude to know what makes the world a better place. When he starts something and sets his mind to it, everything falls into place. His tirelessness and commitment to helping others draw others to his side and cause. People figure if Jon is behind it, it must be the right thing to do. Success follows.

People like Jon make us and the world better just by knowing them. Find the Jon Levys in your world. Support them and learn from them.

## *Straight-A's Culture*

How do Jon and Andy do it? When a customer first enters one of their stores, the employees respond immediately. They really do practice service with a smile. They make you feel you are a somebody. They enact a culture of service and caring. These stores are a great place to go if you need an injection of positive energy, fun, and passion.

An especially handy aspect of their store is their complimentary wrapping service, which is certainly appreciated by customers during the Christmas rush and at birthday-shopping time. Where I live, everyone goes there for birthday presents. How do I know this? Because their wrapping paper keeps turning up everywhere I go.

# NEVER STOP MOVING

*"One way to keep momentum going is to have constantly greater goals."*
— *Michael Korda*

Action is physical. You have to move and just do it. No one else can do it for you. You need to be the person taking that action, learning from it in order to acquire the skills and habits needed in your life journey. The great cyclist Lance Armstrong keeps moving. So do tennis player Martina Navratilova and golfer Tiger Woods. Great athletes are always moving. Great scientists are always moving. Einstein and Edison worked long hours, constantly making progress in the direction of their breakthroughs and success.

You own your success, and take responsibility for it. It's in your hands. It is up to you to put it to action. All the concepts, principles, and ideas discussed in this book must be part of your action steps. You must be in perpetual motion.

Once in motion, the momentum of taking action every day will sustain you. If you stop or quit moving in the direction of your desires, dreams, vision, and passions, then you are in neutral and going nowhere fast. These are not temporary but continuous actions as you master the Straight A's in life.

Exercise is the best motion, especially when starting things off in the morning. As mentioned above, every morning when I wake up, I follow a routine I have been doing for over 20 years. It's simple and has become a habit. I do stretches, 200 crunches, and 150 pushups. This gets my flow going for the day. I start the day off by getting in motion. I am so conditioned by this that if I miss a morning, I feel I am cheating myself and missing a big piece of that day's puzzle.

My brother, David, vowed that he would do at least 30 minutes of exercise every day and has become the Ironman of personal fitness: he is well past 2,000 days without failing to meet his goal. That's 30 minutes, every day, for over five years.

Lance rides his bike. Edison leads his team in experiment after experiment. They lead by example and are successful by example … living their passion … always in motion.

# NEVER STOP NETWORKING

> *"If you want one year of prosperity, grow grain.*
> *If you want ten years of prosperity, grow trees. If you want*
> *one hundred years of prosperity, grow people. "*
> — Harvey Mackay

A great way to start taking action is to understand and implement the power of networking. Simply put, networking is connecting with people. Remember, every time you are in contact with another human being, you are networking. We tend to get preoccupied with the notion that networking is an exercise that's somehow separate from life. Thus we put too much effort into trying to figure out how to do it. If it helps you, throw out the word "networking" altogether and replace it with "people."

> *"A network replaces the weaknesses of the*
> *individual with the strength of the group."*
> — Harvey Mackay

Key factors in the networking game are finding common ground, sharing contacts, and getting to know others and their interests.

The iceberg is a perfect metaphor for networking. It's all about the power of tapping into the vast potential of wealth that exists below the surface.

## How Big Is Your Network?

Think as far back as you can remember. Think about all the people you have ever met. Think about those you met through school, your neighbors, clubs, associations, jobs, camps, volunteer work, your dentist, doctor, real estate broker, car salesman, and so on. Your network is made up of hundreds of people you've known over the years. You may say you've got at least 200. I disagree, because each of those people knows at least another 200 people. Hence your network is at least 40,000.

This may seem like a crazy number. I agree, it is big, but so is your network. I am not saying it's advisable to tap into anywhere close to that number, but the mere fact that there are that many people who conceivably could help you should boost your confidence.

## One to Two Degrees of Separation

The expression "it's a small world" is truer than you can imagine. According to the idea of six degrees of separation, every person on earth is connected to every other person through a chain of acquaintances containing no more than five intermediaries. Depending on whom you know, you may be only four degrees of separation removed from Nelson Mandela, or three from Oprah. Even more amazing, if you want to get to know someone within your city, industry, or community, you are probably only one or two acquaintances away.

Your network is much bigger than you thought! And you're closer to the people in your network than you thought. If you need to meet a particular person, you are only a few steps away. The trick – and the ultimate goal of networking – is to get within one degree of separation of that individual. In the next few pages, we'll see how to do this, by leveraging the power of your network using the Straight A's.

## Double Your Network

> **Networking is a contact sport ... you have to connect with people.**

Anytime you are in a room with a group of people, you can do a powerful exercise that will double your network and point you in the right direction regarding the most important habit and discipline when networking. Have everybody take a minute or two to introduce themselves to at least one person in the room and exchange business cards. As soon as you have finished introducing yourself, spend the next minute telling that person what you could do for them. This is a new twist on telling them about you and focusing on you, which is how it's done most of the time.

Make sure you carry your business cards with you to any networking function or anytime you are in public. You never know whom you will run into. This becomes a good habit if you do it every day. Your cards are your currency in business. Don't leave home for a networking event or session without them.

## Two Powerful Networks in My Life

Two ongoing life experiences have become major networks in my life.

The first is the Taylor Statten Camps in Algonquin Provincial Park in Ontario. I was a camper at this camp from ages nine to sixteen and then spent seven years on staff. I made friends with people from all over the world during my times at the camp, and they continue to be major connections for me through events and reunions.

Many of the people I met when I was as young as nine are still some of my best friends today. They live in Canada and the U.S. When I was in high school, I went to Hawaii for two weeks and stayed with a cabin-mate of mine. Nice part of the world to visit a friend!

After university, I played professional hockey in Europe. A good buddy, whom I met at camp when I was eight years old and who has become one of my closest friends of the past 40 years, came over to Europe to travel with me after the hockey season. Tom and I stayed with friends we went to camp with, at their homes in Hamburg and Rome. The network from this camp is truly global. This incredible bond and common ground we call camp is as strong today as it was four decades ago.

The second major network is Xerox. I worked for that company in the 1990s for five years. Everywhere I go or do business, I continually run into X Men and X Women. Close to 50% of my customers have some tie to my Xerox contacts or have come to me through these contacts. Our common bonds have made, and are making, all the difference in my career.

Camps, companies, community clubs, university alumni groups – these are just a few of the many powerful networks that help us navigate our way to success in life. These are major contributors to how successful you will be as you help others in these networks achieve what they are looking for.

### Successful People

Oprah and Bill Clinton are two very successful people. They are successful today because of their networks. They will both tell you that you get where you want to go through people. Networking is simply connecting with people. Both of these people are incredible givers and networking gurus. They also realize that you can't do it alone and surround themselves with the very best people.

# JOIN THE G7 CLUB

> *"The best way to find yourself*
> *is to lose yourself in the service of others."*
> *– Gandhi*

When you meet with another person for the purpose of networking, you generally fall into the trap of, "What can I get out of this?" This is the first mistake many make. The most successful people give of their time and resources to other people and groups without expecting anything in return. I call this the G7 Club: people who give, give, give, give, give, give ... and give again.

## Giving Is Rule #1

Giving is the essence of networking. It is Rule #1, whether you have a job or not.

Reciprocation may not occur immediately. It may take months or even years. But what goes around comes around and eventually it will come back to you, in one form or another. It is important to note that there is no timeframe for expecting something in return. You must keep an open mind that it will come back at some point.

> *"We make a living by what we get,*
> *but we make a life by what we give."*
> *– Winston Churchill*

It's not easy giving all the time; it takes practice. But once you have mastered this philosophy, you will always be in the giving mode. You will always have the giving attitude.

## Make Their Day

When you first meet someone, pretend they have an imaginary sign around their neck that says, "Make me feel important ... make me feel good." Or, if you subscribe to the Clint Eastwood school of networking, the sign would read, "Make my day." In other words, make their day! If you understand that it is about the other person, you will be successful in every encounter. It's always all about them. Let them do the talking. You ask the questions, and listen carefully to their answers.

You should also find out what's important to the other person. You can then send them a little gift relating to their particular interest, whether it's a book, an article, or even a CD. Additionally, you may want to try to introduce them to someone else who has similar interests. You can help people out in so many ways if you take the time to understand their interests and how you can help them.

Here are some of the gifts you can give, whether they are something you purchase, or, even more powerfully, are gifts of yourself:

- Books
- Being present
- Being focused on what people are saying
- Just listening
- Giving compliments
- Being polite
- Repeating what people say to you to let them know you heard them
- Sending an article of interest
- Sending a birthday email
- Sending them a card at Christmas or New Year's
- Introducing them to people you think they can help or who would be good contacts for them

## Pay It Forward

In the movie *Pay It Forward*, a young boy figures out, through a school assignment he chooses, that if he helps three people and they help three people and so on, eventually everyone on the planet will be part of the cause and the world will be a better place. This concept takes off and starts a flood of people helping other people with no expectation of being paid back.

This is the way powerful and far-reaching networks are built. Just remember to pay it forward. Rent this movie. Besides being great entertainment, it will give you one of the greatest lessons in life on giving. The secret is to pay it forward, and to keep on paying it forward.

## Corkism #1

Forgive my Dr. Seuss-like wording, but I find his approach the best way to explain some key points. First, fill in the blank:

"It's not what you know, but _____."

The answer, of course, is: "... it's who you know."

I will use a little bit of my background of reading lots of Dr. Seuss to explain this in greater detail.

Some people know lots of things. Other people know lots of people. Now, if we could connect the two groups ... look out! **It's not just what you know and it's not just who you know. It's what you know about who you know.**

You have to spend the time to get to know what's important to other people, to know what makes them feel good about life. This is what's below the surface of their lives and what will make all the difference to them.

### *Straight to My Heart*

If someone comes up to me and says, "How are your kids Stephanie and Geoffrey?" I am impressed. I know they have taken the time to get to know a little bit about me. Since my children happen to be more important to me than anything else, the person has scored big time with me.

As mentioned above, people want to feel how much you care and know. You have to start with the knowing first, though, then start a relationship and build that trust to help break down any barriers. The more you know about the other person, the more it shows you care.

## You Can't Be the Expert in Everything

I have often talked about how, in today's world, there are experts and specialists in everything. If you need someone to fix a broken door or the lock on a door, you probably have to contact separate people who are specialists in each of these tasks. Only once you use both have you completely repaired the door.

You don't need to know everything. In fact, no one can know everything. One person can have great depths of knowledge in many areas, but that doesn't mean they know everything. You may not even be interested in trying to learn everything. So why not call an expert when you need something out of your area of expertise? Consult your network. Most companies work on the premise of having people with different skill sets working together as a whole to get the job done. This can work for you personally, too.

One day, when I was driving my daughter, Stephanie, to school, she said she didn't see why she had to go to school and study so hard. As I began my protest, I got the feeling that she was about to hit me with the old, "But Dad, you said ..." Sure enough, she reminded me that there are people who specialize and become experts in certain areas. "I can just tap into the people around me," she said, with a smirk.

She's right, overall, but in the case of knowledge, we are cheating ourselves not to learn as much as we can. In school we are building a foundation of knowledge, which we will tap into and build on for the rest of our lives. This at least gives us a snapshot of the knowledge we need – often from experts – in order to understand certain situations or meet certain goals.

## Corkism #2

**It's not just what you know or what you know about whom you know. It's what you do with what you know about whom you know ... you know?**

In other words, you have to take action. It's the combination of the Straight A's that makes the difference.

People are always talking about connections. My thought on connections is that if you don't use or leverage a connection, then it's not really a connection. When you know someone who can help you get to where you want to go, you have to contact them, connect with them, and ask for their help, direction, or support.

## Write It Down

When you make a connection, write down what you need to remember. When we write something down, our retention level goes up by 50%. That alone is a good enough reason to follow this practice. As I mentioned earlier in the book, the more senses you can juice, the greater the impression on you and the more you will remember. Writing introduces one of our most important senses – touch – and helps us be that much more efficient and effective.

Out of courtesy, ask the person you are meeting if you may take notes. They will undoubtedly say yes. It's not like what they're saying is top secret.

Do not rely on your memory; it will let you down. Our minds work much more quickly than any other part of our bodies. We can never catch up or record everything we're thinking of, but at least by writing it down we will have *some* record to draw on when we need it. Have a sheet with questions already written down to help jog your memory and ensure that you get the information you need. Once you record things, you can continue to build on that knowledge.

Writing down information while in front of someone shows them that you are interested in what they are saying. It makes them feel good that you are documenting their comments. You should always transfer this information to an electronic database, so you can easily access it and continue to build on it.

Take the time to record people's interests, hobbies, work history, family ... what's important to them. By doing this, you remove barriers to relationship building. This is how a powerful and long relationship is built. It shows you care when you record information and keep a record of it.

It certainly makes a huge impression on me when someone comes to a meeting prepared in this way.

# THE ELEVATOR SPEECH

You must always be prepared to answer people when they ask you how you are, or what you do for a living. This can come up anytime, anywhere.

Most people, when they are asked what they do for a living or what they bring to the table, have a hard time articulating it. People spend very little time on their "brand me" speech and how to state it powerfully and quickly.

## Only 30 Seconds

The average human attention span is approximately 30 seconds. Advertisers have figured this out. They have done their homework – billions of dollars worth. That's why the average TV commercial runs between 15 and 30 seconds.

This is true for you, too. It is critical that you determine the right length and approach of every message you deliver.

One way to do this is to develop and practice what's called an elevator speech: a message you can get across to someone in the time it takes to get from the main floor to your office in an elevator.

Take time to master your 30-second speech for your product, service, or yourself. Once you understand that you only have a few seconds to make your point, you can focus on what will really promote you, or the exact message you want to get across.

## Seven Steps to a Great Elevator Speech

The first step is to write down your message. Your elevator speech must have a bit of an intro, some meat in the middle, and then an ending that's short, clean, and concise. The main objective every time is to create some interest, pique their curiosity, and introduce a hook so they want more. If it works for you, keep doing it or saying what you're saying. Check for the response. If what you're saying doesn't work, then you have to change it up, modifying and expanding as needed.

After you write down your 30-second speech, you should then break it down to bullets. These bullets will be what you use to remind yourself of what you're saying. If you rattled off a memorized speech or were to read it, your audience would deem your message futile and ignore it. That's how we treat telemarketers! Creating bullet points will help you sound genuine. Your message needs to come straight from the heart. It will allow you to rework your message every time you use it, so that it sounds fresh.

Then it's time to practice your speech. Take it for a few trial spins on the telephone and in front of family members or friends; rewrite it based on the feedback you're getting; practice it some more and then ... practice it some more! All this will serve to help you develop confidence in your speech, feel good about it, and sound natural in delivering it.

## *The Seven Steps*

1) Write it down
2) Put into bullet form/refine
3) Practice
4) Try it on people, live and by phone
5) Rewrite it
6) Practice some more
7) Rehearse it again and again

# THE ART OF
# COLD CALLING

Keep the following in mind when you are cold-calling someone to try to meet with them:

- 50% of people quit calling after the first call
- 80% after the second
- 90% after the third
- 97% after the fourth

So the magic number, then, is to call at least five times. If you keep calling, you are eliminating most of the other people trying to meet with that person, because they belong to the categories above. Another rule of thumb is that 80% of business is done after five calls.

## When to Stop

I don't believe you ever stop calling, especially if you are really determined to meet with someone. Keep calling. Remember to use all the strategies. As I said earlier in this book, what are people going to do, tell you to stop being so polite?

Generally you know how good a good friend is by how quickly they answer your phone calls. Yet, sometimes, in this chaotic world of ours, even a good friend will fail to do so.

I remember once when one of my friends was not returning my calls. I left him a message, then a week later another one, and then two weeks later another one. For the following three months I called every two weeks. I was trying to get him to do some business with my company.

Finally even I was getting frustrated. I decided to stop calling, thinking that he just didn't care or was too busy to talk to me. (I know, I know: slow reflexes, Cork.)

A month later he called me. The first thing he said was, "Tim, I admire your persistence."

Most people do, if you do it right.

He went on to say he had been very busy and had recently been promoted and now could send more business my way.

This sort of thing happens all the time. I've seen it over the years in sales and running large sales organizations. People give up just short of hitting the jackpot. Someone else who has had more determination and persistence hits it instead.

## Avoid Putting Them on the Spot

When you're asking for contacts from people you don't know very well, it can be awkward for both of you. This is a real art. You have to be able to read people well and know when to back off and try a more subtle approach. First of all, you have to earn the right to ask and very rarely will they give up a few contacts before they get to know and trust you. Also, by asking them "live," they may feel put on the spot and may not be able to remember any contacts. As soon as there is any hesitation, you may want to suggest you will email them, in order to give them some time to think about it. This also gives them time to decide whether they want to help and doubles as a professional, courteous approach.

When you do email them, ask if they could provide you with one or two contacts that may help you in your quest.

## Make It Warm

When people agree to help you meet someone else, ask them to please put a call in to that person to warm things up. This will make life a lot easier for you when you make the call. Another helpful thing to do is volunteer what they could say when they call the person to introduce you. This helps them in their busy schedules and it will ensure that they articulate the message the way you want it expressed. Warm is always better than cold. Networking helps skip a few steps by having people help you get in the door much faster and friendlier.

## Follow Up

I have experienced countless times when following up with polite persistence made a big difference.

One example involves a top-five Canadian bank that I spent three years trying to get as a customer. Are you ready for this? (I kept a log.) I made 78 phone calls, nine presentations, and met with 27 different people on the way to securing the business.

> **You are your own umpire in life. Only you can call yourself out. Don't call yourself out. Let them say no.**

I recall another situation where it took six months to get the business, I met with eighteen different people and made 39 phone calls and four presentations. And get this: This was all after meeting with the president first and getting his blessing. Furthermore, I had previously worked for this company, for five years, and knew all the key decision makers.

The reason I met so many people was to get buy-in from all the different stakeholders and influencers – which is critical in setting up any lasting partnership in business.

## Use emails

Always send an email within 24 hours. The more quickly you get back to someone, the more impressive. I do recommend you do this at the end of the day for any meeting you had, whether it was in person or on the phone. Make it a habit, especially when you were the one who initiated the meeting.

In the subject line of the email, write, "Thank You for Your Time." There is nothing more valuable than a person's time. Make the message short and sweet, never more than two short paragraphs. If it is too long they won't read it. End it with good wishes. I always finish mine off with, "Have a Great Day!"

## Send Thank-you cards

I am a big believer in sending thank-you cards. In the world of email, cards are a rarity. Because of the time expectations that have been ingrained into us, given today's instant communications, we have lost the art of sending these cards.

I think sending an email *and* a thank-you card is ideal. People will appreciate an email because they expect speed. But they will appreciate a card, too, because … very few people take the time to send them anymore! You need to do both to make a real impact. I love receiving a handwritten card. It is much more personal and leaves a lasting impression.

# Fly with the Eagles

If you want to fly with the eagles, you have to hang out with them and find out what they do that gets them to such great heights. The eagles are those who have already achieved lofty heights. They are the influencers who can help you get where you want to go. You want to find out from them how they did it and what made them successful. What their journey was and how they handled the trials and tribulations through their success, failure, rejection, and fears.

Wherever you want to go or whatever you want to do, there is a good chance the eagles have gone that way before. Ask them to spend some time with you. Approach even the loftiest of them. Most are more approachable than you imagine. Do your homework and find out some of their accomplishments and the history of their achievements. Then use that information to get their attention. Get them talking about themselves. Make them feel good and important … make their day!

To get someone's attention or get them to return your call, you must pique their interest or curiosity.

Let the eagles know you admire them or remember something they did and that you would like their advice on something. If they say no, which they may, move to the next one. Don't spend too much time on them if they aren't open to helping. I suspect that those who refuse to help are not true eagles. The most powerful attribute and number-one rule to flying high in the world is to give. To help people when they ask for it is the purest way to give. The true eagles will always take the time to give you a few lessons on how to soar.

## The 80-20 Rule

The 80-20 Rule was formulated at the turn of the 20th century by an Italian named Vilfredo Pareto. It covers the many situations where 80% of the consequences come from 20% of the causes. For example, in many companies 80% of their business is generated by 20% of their staff – their top performers – or 80% of their income comes from 20% of their customers.

It works in a similar way when it comes to success. There's always a certain small group who are the main influencers. They are the eagles, the go-to performers you want to imitate.

The rule can also be reversed. People have a tendency in whatever they are doing to spend 80% of their time on the 80% that only produces 20%. The key to success in life and business is to spend 80% of your time on the 20% that will give you 80%. Businesses should spend most of their time on the small percentage of customers who give them the majority of their business, but they don't.

In the future, think about that top 20% and focus most of your effort there. Your business and personal life will reap the benefits.

# SET THE RIGHT GOALS

> *"The greater danger for most of us lies not in setting our aim too high and falling short, but in setting our aim too low and achieving our mark."*
> – *Michelangelo*

| |
|---|
| **Goals are critical to success, but until you take action, they can't be achieved.** |

Do you have goals? Do you write them down? Do you review them once a day or once a week? Goal-setting is one of the most critical skills to master in creating success in your life. It's a skill that you can learn. I am motivated, consoled, or calmed by thinking of what's really important in my life.

## Your Future by Design

Our lives are the result of our choices. To blame and accuse other people, the environment in which we live, or other external influences is to choose to empower the things that control us. We are doing the choosing – either to live our lives or to let others live them for us. By making and keeping promises to ourselves and others, little by little we increase our strength until our ability to act is more powerful than any other forces that act on us.

The best way to predict your future is to create it. Just as you can use the power of creative imagination to see a goal before you accomplish it, so you can imagine your own reality before you live it.

## Add Goals to Your Journal

A journal is a great place to keep your goals so they are always accessible. Rewrite them every six months to stay current (they should always be evolving in response to the changes in your circumstances). You can keep your short-range, mid-range, and long-range goals in these journals. When you look at them from the vantage-point of months and years, you will see what goals you had at certain stages in your life. As already mentioned in this book, I have been keeping journals for over eighteen years. I enjoy going back occasionally to see what drove and motivated me in years gone by. It is important to date your goals and journals so you can build from your past successes and experience.

### And the Survey Says ...

Many studies have been done on whether setting goals and writing goals down makes a difference to people's success. In one university, survey organizers asked the graduating class which of them set goals and who wrote them down. Only 15% of them could even describe any goals they had for themselves, and even fewer – 3% – not only had them but also wrote them down.

The statistic that really had an impact was that many years later, the 3% who wrote their goals down were worth more than the other 97% combined. But is this so extraordinary? No, it's reality.

If you don't have goals for yourself and don't write them down, and if you don't have a system for reviewing your goals and holding yourself accountable to reach them, then, like most of the population, you're going to spend your life living out someone else's goals.

## Why People Don't Set Goals

There are three main reasons that people don't set goals: not achieving the Straight A's of attitude, aptitude, and action. And there are three main reasons they don't achieve these goals: fear, rejection, and fail-

> **Success is a journey AND a destination.**

ure. We know through the Straight-A's philosophy that these latter three reasons are deterrents to success. Those who overcome the deterrents are successful and reach great heights in their endeavors in all areas of life, personally, in their health, in their business, in their charitable work. These people all realize that these three deterrents are indispensable prerequisites for success. The more we learn through them, the more successful we can become.

## Reversing Rejection

Fear can keep us in check. But rejection is a big part of success because reversing it makes us a success. Failure is only failure if we fail to learn from it and improve for the next time. Experiencing failure can give us the resolve and knowledge to try again to challenge adversity and eventually triumph.

Then there is doubt, which many times is directed at us by family or even our best friends. How often do we hear someone – a co-worker, family member, or even friends – say, "You can't do that. What are you thinking?"

After enough people say that, you can start to believe it.

### *Goals and Self-confidence*

The greatest deterrent to success is lack of self-confidence. This comes from not doing what you are capable of doing. Setting goals and then achieving them is therefore a huge boost to self-confidence and self-esteem. Setting and achieving goals makes you feel good about you and is the foundation of confidence. When you're feeling good about yourself, everything seems easier to accomplish.

# CREATE A GOAL
# ACTION PLAN

> *"You miss 100% of the shots you don't take."*
> — *Wayne Gretzky*

What is your goal action plan and when are you going to sign up to put it into action? You can find a partner, coach, or mentor to hold you accountable. I have hired a coach numerous times in my career. Often I have partnered with someone so the two of us can hold each other accountable. We drive each other to action. The two of us have a contract in which both of us agree to help the other achieve daily or annual goals and disciplines. Sometimes we need the extra push to get us moving in the right direction. A little friendly competition doesn't hurt, either.

## Your Annual Goals

The worksheets that follow are a sample of what you could use to record your goals for the year.

Fill the first chart out quickly, putting down your major goals for the year. Write a few in each area. Take about ten minutes to fill it in. This is the big-picture record of your goals and aspirations. Keep it simple and easy to read. Don't write too many goals. Record your top two or three goals in each of these main areas in your life. Sign this chart, date it, put it in an envelope, and seal it. Don't look at it for a year or, if you prefer, at the next turn of the year.

Fill the second chart out with more precision, because here you are going on record regarding the daily habits and disciplines you are going to follow to reach these short-term goals. Meeting these day-by-day goals will enable you to reach your long-range goals. This is your map for staying on course. You will need to review this chart weekly in order to measure your progress. This will have a powerful effect in helping you achieve your major goals throughout the year. You will be surprised at how your short-term disciplines will help you reach your long-term goals.

Repeat the exercise for the next year!

## MY ANNUAL GOALS FOR _____

FAMILY & PERSONAL

_____
_____
_____
_____

HEALTH & FITNESS

_____
_____
_____
_____

CAREER

_____
_____
_____
_____

FINANCIAL

_____
_____
_____
_____

OTHER

_____
_____
_____
_____

NAME: _____

DATE: _____

## MY ANNUAL GOALS FOR _____

### SUCCESS IS A CHOICE ...

FAMILY & PERSONAL

_____
_____
_____
_____
_____
_____
_____
_____

HEALTH – FITNESS
& WELLNESS

_____
_____
_____
_____
_____
_____
_____

CAREER

_____
_____
_____
_____
_____
_____
_____
_____

FINANCIAL

_____
_____
_____
_____
_____
_____
_____

SELF-IMPROVEMENT
& EDUCATION

_____
_____
_____
_____
_____
_____
_____
_____

OTHER

_____
_____
_____
_____
_____
_____
_____

DATE: _____

Write your goals as if you have already achieved them. Present tense, positive. This will lock them into your mind.

### Goals Should be SMART ———————————————————

S = Specific
M = Measurable
A = Assignable (who does what)
R = Realistic
T = Time-based

# ACHIEVE YOUR GOALS

> *"Success is nothing more than a few simple disciplines practiced every day."*
> — Jim Rohn

In setting and achieving your goals, the law of the farm prevails, as Stephen Covey points out in his book *The Seven Habits of Highly Effective People.* In other words, you must plant the seeds, nurture them, and then harvest when the produce is ready. You cannot skip any of these steps or you will not succeed. These are natural laws. You have to follow the same laws again and again and continually harvest the rewards. You can't cheat the process.

Another way to state this is as the law of sowing and reaping. You reap what you sow — you get what you give. The same law applies in setting and achieving your goals. You plant the seeds of opportunity by setting goals. Then you nurture your goals by following a process to attain them. Eventually you take action, reaping what you have sown.

## Practicing Good Habits

Appetite is an instinctive human trait that is automatic ... it just happens ... it is hardwired into our systems. These appetites will control us unless we program ourselves to make a virtue of them so they become daily habits. The trick is to figure out what the good habits are and program them into our minds and bodies.

Good habits are indispensable to reaching our goals because they give us the day-to-day disciplines that enable us to reach them. As we working toward our goals by practicing the fundamentals every day, we are making our habits instinctive.

Tony Robbins developed an audio series about ten years ago that focused on habits. The tapes ran three weeks and you were supposed to listen to so much every day for 30 days. Tony understands what making and breaking habits is all about. He is the

> **Eighty percent of what you do every day is a habit.**

master teacher and his tape series on creating good habits is very powerful. When we repeat something for a number of days in a row, it becomes a habit and is instinctive every day.

> **"We are what we repeatedly do.**
> **Excellence, then, is not an act, but a habit."**
> *– Aristotle*

So if we can focus on practicing fundamental disciplines, we will be creating the habits that help us become extremely successful in life. Following are the major ones that have had a huge impact on my life.

## My Top Sixteen Habits

1) Call two new people every day
2) Get up at 6 a.m. and be at work by 8 a.m.
3) Make my toughest calls first, and at least five calls before 9 a.m.
4) Plan the next day the night before
5) Make a to-do list every day (use A, B, and C categories)
6) Read for one hour every day
7) Review goals daily
8) Smile
9) Return calls and emails promptly (calls within 24 hours and emails within two days is my rule of thumb)
10) Listen
11) Compliment others and be genuine
12) Don't take myself too seriously
13) When meeting someone, try to repeat their name a few times in the initial conversation in order to remember it
14) Help others help themselves
15) Be game ready at all times
16) Practice PFF (Prospect, Face time, Follow-up)

## Positive Affirmations

Talking to yourself and reaffirming yourself again and again is another key to successfully accomplishing goals. I always like to spend time before I speak to large groups reaffirming myself. I go through a ritual in which I motivate myself by repeating over and over again in my mind that I am going to do a great job and wow the audience. Sometimes I look in the mirror as I say this or walk around the room. I think positive thoughts and mentally walk myself through my speech, imagining myself wowing the crowd and receiving their affirmation.

## PFF (Prospect, Face time, Follow-up)

I have used PFF for 25 years. It's a reminder to me that my main focus should always be to get face time. My goal is to meet people whom I can help, or who can help me, or those to whom I can offer my company's services. Every person who is doing any sort of business development, sales, or marketing and has any interaction with potential customers has to make PFF a habit.

The most important part of this habit is spending more than two hours per day on it. Why more than two hours? Because statistics tell us that most people spend about two hours on it. Just fifteen minutes more than what they are doing will get you out of the pool of mediocrity!

This rule applies to anyone in career transition and searching for a job. My question to you, if you are not spending at least three or four hours a day in the PFF mode, is what are you doing with your time? This is where you have to focus. There is no substitute!

# PRACTICE THE FUNDAMENTALS

> *"Success is neither magical nor mysterious. Success is the natural consequence of consistently applying the basic fundamentals."*
> *– Jim Rohn*

To achieve your goals, you must practice the fundamentals every day.

Michael Jordan practiced harder than anyone else on his team. He was usually the first on the court and the last off. He did this in high school, going on to realize his dream of playing college basketball – and of playing in the NBA.

Steffi Graf practiced hard her whole tennis career. She was naturally gifted, but her hard work on the fundamentals day after day took her to the top of women's tennis. She was one of the greatest ever to play the game.

Wayne Gretzky started playing hockey at a very young age and played for hours day after day as a kid and on into his adult years. He worked hard at the basics. His dad used to spend countless hours working with him.

Tiger Woods is another person who excels at the basics. He admits that he works on his golf game harder than anyone else. Even though he has dominated the world golf scene for the past decade, he has coaches work with him on every part of his game.

## Back to Basics

The common denominator for all these great athletes is they all excel at the fundamentals. I don't for a second believe that they aren't extremely talented athletes, but their tireless work ethic to excel and practice harder than anyone else is what makes the difference for them.

Great athletes and coaches will tell you that the fundamentals are what have made them successful. Think about the greatest coaches in history (Vince Lombardi, John Wooden, Scottie Bowman, among others). These individuals are best known for teaching the fundamentals, even though their pupils were already the best in the world at what they did, for their age.

One of the most successful coaches of all time is John Wooden, who coached the UCLA Bruins basketball team to ten national titles. He won seven of them in a row. This was unprecedented and no coach at this level has come anywhere close. It's tough enough just to repeat a championship: when you win three or four they call your team a dynasty.

Wooden was asked what the main factor was that contributed to his success. He said it was getting his athletes to practice the fundamentals. Asked how he defined the fundamentals, he described what he did with his players to make them so successful year after year.

When training camp started, he would bring the players out on the court and ask them to shoot a few baskets. Then he would start working with individual players. He would take one and have him take a shot from a certain position. Then Wooden would say, "Now do it 300 times."

Then he would take the player to a different spot on the court and say, "Shoot from here." Then he'd say, "Now do it 300 times."

After a few weeks, the players would always ask if they could let up on this exercise. After all, they were some of the best players in the world and were practicing harder then anyone else.

"No," Wooden would say. "When there are only three seconds left in the game and the national championship is on the line, I don't want you to have to think about it; you will just shoot and, swish, the ball will go in the hoop."

This is true in everything we do in life. We are successful because we become experts at what we do through excelling in the fundamentals at work, in our family, our health, sports, the charities we give to. We become experts through working hard on those areas, learning through experience, both in failure and success.

> **Fact: You must be an obsessive goal-setter to achieve greatness!**

# KEEP ON SWINGING

*"Being defeated is often a temporary condition.*
*Giving up is what makes it permanent."*
– Marilyn vos Savant

In major league baseball, the best hitters strike out on average seven out of every ten times they face the pitcher. They don't even make it to first base seven out of ten times they walk up to that plate. But they don't look at it that way. If you actually get to first base three out of the ten times and your lifetime batting average is over .300, then you are probably going to end up in the Baseball Hall of Fame.

It's the same in life. You are going to fail and strike out a much higher percentage of the time than you are going to get a hit – not to mention a home run.

Babe Ruth was one of the greatest hitters in baseball. He also struck out a high percentage of the time. Yet he went on to be one of the greatest athletes and celebrities of the 20th century. His attitude was to go for the fence every time. In one famous incident when he was at bat, he pointed to a wall just before the pitch was delivered and then proceeded to hit it over that wall. Call it arrogance, confidence, or whatever you will, but he had the belief and the passion as well as the ability.

But even the Babe knew he would fail to get a hit most of the time. It simply didn't matter. He just kept swinging.

As long as you are willing to stand there long enough and swing often and hard enough, you will eventually hit it out of the park. In the process, you will get to first some of the time, or maybe halfway home with a double. Sometimes you will be walked or given a free base.

But whatever base you reach, and however you reach it, you must realize that the journey is not over. You may occasionally have to take a risk and steal second. You may be stranded on base as other hitters fail to connect with the ball.

## You Are Your Own Umpire

If you do decide to take the risks necessary to get to the next base, you have to do your homework, evaluate the odds, and be perceptive. Find your opening. In the baseball game of life, you are your own umpire. You decide whether you are safe or out. You have the ability to call yourself out, or to do as Babe Ruth did and just keep swinging.

If you are in sales, for example, you are not always going to have success when calling on customers. Most of the time you will be rejected and failure will be the outcome. Did you learn in the process? Every time you learn a little more, success will be that much closer, until it's just around the corner – and then, yes, there it is!

## Welcoming Failure

Some people in sales have a refreshing attitude toward failure. They are happy to rack up a high number of failures in their jobs. Why? Because they know that when they reach a certain number of rejections per day or per week, they're that much closer to a success.

In other words, their attitude is, "Bring it on!"

---

### *Speed Bumps or Walls?*

People who give up too easily see obstacles in their lives as walls. After a while, these walls just look insurmountable to them.

Others have a much better spin on obstacles. They see them as speed bumps. Speed bumps slow them down and make them careful not to hurt others and themselves. But they're still getting somewhere!

It's all in your attitude and perception.

# KEEP A SCORECARD

Anything can happen in life – it's how you react that counts. When you get a deal or win business or achieve an objective, keep a scorecard on what you learned and the behaviors you noticed. You should repeat those behaviors to ensure success again. You should also keep track when you lose business so you can learn from your mistakes. You have the opportunity to take corrective action since the real reasons are staring you right in the face.

This approach can be very telling. Scorecards help you understand successes. They also help you highlight failures, which helps you to not repeat them. By mapping information through a scorecard, you can get the facts.

Use a form like the one below to keep track of goals that you have achieved or failed to achieve. Ask yourself why you achieved a certain goal, or why you didn't.

*"Develop a passion for learning.*
*If you do, you will never cease to grow."*
– Anthony J. D'Angelo

| Goal | Achieved Lessons Learned | Not Achieved Lessons Learned |
|---|---|---|
|  |  |  |
|  |  |  |
|  |  |  |
|  |  |  |
|  |  |  |

Another type of daily scorecard that is very effective is shown below. I have a form like this in the daily planner that I designed years ago. I keep score of how many of these items I conduct.

| Activity | # |
|---|---|
| Warm calls | |
| Cold calls | |
| Emails | |
| Presentations | |
| Contacts/Database | |
| Networking | |

This scorecard drives me to act in each area. It is a constant reminder, helping me hold myself accountable. It also plays on the fact that I like to see and keep track of my daily accomplishments. Have I made the effort? Each check mark or point I get beside each activity motivates me just like when I was a student and my teacher gave me stars for good behavior. It also allows me to see what I do daily and whether I adhered to core activities and disciplines.

This simple tool drives success for me and my company. Ultimately, keeping score in this way keeps me focused on my objectives and goals while providing me with a snapshot of my daily success.

# TAKE THE RISK

Opportunity always involves risk. You can't keep your foot on first and steal second. If you don't take the risk, which is very important when trying to attain your goals, you can't take your game to a new level. Calculated risk is an essential part of the game.

## Three Types of People

There are three types of people in this world. People who make things happen. People who watch things happen. And, finally, poeple who wonder, what happened? Don't be in the last category.

*"Accept the challenges, so you may feel the exhilaration of victory."*
— George S. Patton

By taking action you are never wondering what happened. By taking action you are making things happen. Don't sit on the bench or in the crowd too often. If you get the chance to sit it out or dance ... dance!

## Three Magic Letters: A. S. K.

Setting your goals is one thing. To attain what you want, you must take another risk – the risk of being brave enough to show your lack of knowledge by asking questions.

Ask questions. Ask why, ask why not, ask how, ask who, ask where, ask when, ask what, ask. When you ask, you get yourself out of the land of uncertainty and into yes or no. Asking creates clarity.

# MAKE A DIFFERENCE

Last year at ABC Sales Inc., Susan was the top salesperson for the third year in a row. As a reward and in appreciation for her great performance and consistent behavior, she was sent on an all-expenses-paid trip to Nassau in the Bahamas.

The first morning she arose at seven o'clock and enjoyed a leisurely breakfast overlooking the beach, sitting under a bright blue sky. Looking out at the beach, she noticed a man collecting starfish and throwing them back in the ocean one by one. This seemed kind of odd, because there were thousands of starfish on the beach and he wasn't making much of a dent in his task. She went back to her breakfast and didn't give it a second thought.

*"Always use the word 'impossible' with the greatest caution."*
— *Wernher von Braun*

The next morning she rose early again and went for the same walk on the same beach. Again she noticed the same old man walking up and down the beach for hours throwing the starfish that had washed back on the beach back into the ocean one at a time. She was getting curious, but let it go.

The next morning, same routine and the same scene. This was just too much for her to take. Her curiosity getting the better of her, she walked down to the beach to talk to the old man.

"Why do you go on throwing starfish back in the ocean hour after hour, day after day, when they're just going to end up washing back up on the beach by the thousands?" she asked.

"Ah, but young lady I am making a difference," the old man said.

She looked puzzled and asked how.

> **We all can make a difference, one person at a time, one customer at a time.**

With that the old man picked up a starfish looked Susan in the eye. "It makes a difference to this one," he said and proceeded to throw the starfish back into the ocean.

(An adaptation of Loren Eisley's famous story, from *The Star Thrower*.)

## *Terry and Rick*

Two incredible examples of determination and persistence are Terry Fox and Rick Hansen. They have made a huge difference to people all over the world.

At age nineteen, Terry was diagnosed with cancer in his knee and had to have his leg amputated from just above his knee. While in the hospital, he saw many people of all ages suffering and dying from cancer and decided he had to make a difference. He resolved to run across Canada.

Terry started his run in April 1980, running close to a marathon a day for over four months. He would have kept going, but the cancer spread and forced him to stop. He died six months later. Terry ended up going 3,339 miles in total.

He was a true hero, an example of the purest form of determination and persistence. How can you not admire what he did? He did reach his goal of raising over $24 million – one dollar per Canadian – before he died.

> **The race is not always to the swift, but to those who keep on running ... or rolling!**

Now, every September, all over the world, Terry Fox runs are held to pay tribute to him and raise money for cancer research. To date, over $360 million has been raised through his foundation.

Rick Hansen was inspired by Terry Fox. Rick, another Canadian, was thrown from the back of a pickup truck in 1973 when he was fifteen and it left him a paraplegic. In 1977, Terry Fox joined Hansen on the Canadian Wheelchair Foundation. Hansen ran the program.

Rick decided he wanted to do something to make a difference and raise money and awareness for spinal-cord research. In 1985 he circled the globe in his wheelchair. He raised over $26 million and as of today has raised over $158 million. He took on a challenge and achieved a lot more than even he expected.

Rick and Terry are great examples of the Straight A's working in harmony. No obstacles are too big for people with their kind of attitude, aptitude, and actions.

## PART FOUR

# GETTING STRAIGHT A'S

Dream & Visualize

Set a Timeline

Feel the Passion

Overcome Obstacles

Believe

Identify Knowledge Needed

Write It Down

Make a Plan

Analyze Where You Are

Persist!

# THE TEN STEPS TO GETTING STRAIGHT A'S

> *"Success is not the key to happiness. Happiness is the key to success. If you love what you are doing, you will be successful."*
> – *Albert Schweitzer*

The following steps are not the only ones out there but represent the collective wisdom of many experts and 20 years of my own research and practice. These steps are a proven formula for success and will take you to new heights in your journey. If you continually practice and master all ten, you will be in the top 3% to 5% of the population, the success bracket. If you can do at least half of them on a regular basis, you will separate yourself from the crowd. If you are only doing a few of these on a regular basis, you are spending your life on other people's goals, not your own.

## The Ten Steps

### 1. Dream and visualize

You must dream and visualize your goals as if they have already been attained. All great successes lie in dreaming. The vision to see the end from the beginning makes it impossible not to achieve it. Your vision is detailed description of where you want to be. What does your destination look like and feel like?

Paint the picture in your mind again and again, over and over. The more you think about it, the more precise it will become. Your perception becomes reality. Your reality is the ability to dream it, visualize it and then take action and do it. If you can dream it, you can become it.

### 2. Feel the passion

Passion or desire is the great motivator and passion is the fuel that powers you. These are the two major forces drawing you to your goals. They determine that it must be something you really want. You have to make it personal. True desire and passion create a strong, genuine enthusiasm that captures us and drives us toward our goals.

People have incredible passion and desire when they are doing what they love to do and motivated by a task, job, action, vision, or dream. When you have pure passion, it is contagious and generates excitement and energy. People will be drawn in by your passion and desire. The law of attraction will be ignited.

## 3. Believe

You have to believe beyond a shadow of doubt that your goals are achievable. It is not a matter of if, but when. Don't set the bar too high. You don't want the goal to be too hard to achieve. It has to be challenging, but realistic. Move outside your comfort zone and take some risks. Without risks you will spend most of your time in the land of mediocrity where the average play. The conscious mind will accept what it is fed to it by your subconscious mind.

## 4. Write it down

It is absolutely essential that you write down all your goals on a regular basis and revisit and rewrite them every few months, because they are ever-evolving. Writing your goals down will program your subconscious so that you're hard-wired to accomplish them. If you do this every day, it will becomes part of your daily routine, which should be the goal for our goals.

Write in complete detail so you know exactly what it is you are trying to do. Until it is committed to paper, it's not a goal but just a wish. Writing it down makes it real and tangible. It's true when they say out of sight, out of mind. Keep it in plain view. Your retention level goes up by 50% when you write it down. This alone is a great reason to write goals down

## 5. Analyze where you are

Where do you start? Simple: where you are right now. Measure your current status. For example, look at your current income as the starting point and then set your goal to where you want to be in the next year, month, or week. Like Thomas Edison, the writer Stephen Covey promotes a philosophy of starting with the end in mind. He knows that if you set the target, the only thing stopping you from getting there is not taking action. Balance is a huge part of creating harmony and synergy in your life. The areas under which I categorize my goals are:

- Health and Fitness
- Family and Personal

- Career/work
- Financial
- Spiritual
- Other

In each of these areas, I try to put down my five biggest goals for the next year and review them on a regular basis, at least once or twice a week. Break your goals down and celebrate each step you take, building on each success.

## 6. Set a deadline/timeline

When will it be accomplished? What is the latest date? Your goals should be specific and quantifiable. Time is a funny thing. It's the one thing you can't replace once you use it.

You may say you can't afford the time to set goals, but in reality, it's just the opposite: you can't afford not to. Whether you have time is your choice. You choose what to do with your time. You have the time but you just may not want to spend it doing certain things. Focus on one thing at a time and finish it. Stay with it until completion. Do it the first time. Don't procrastinate. Do it now. You are your manager and organizer. Chart your progress. Set priorities and determine what the most valuable use of your time is right now.

## 7. Identify obstacles to overcome

There are always obstacles … 10% of your life is what happens to you and 90% is how you react. Figure out what these obstacles are and resolve to walk right through them with the knowledge of what you need to effectively move to the next step. I believe there are no walls in life, only speed bumps. Some of these speed bumps can be quite large and can come one after another as if they're never going to end.

But you do have what it takes! As Dr. Seuss says, it's "98 and ¾ percent guaranteed" that you will succeed.

Write your problems down. Problems become less urgent when you put them on paper. Writing them down lets you better digest the situation, juice more of your senses, and take the time to think things through, step by step. Identify and prioritize which obstacles to tackle first. Take the attitude that failure is part of the success equation – it helps you learn what not to do the next time.

## 8. Identify knowledge needed

What do you need to help you achieve your goals and make your journey successful. Read the books. Everything you need to know is in a book some-where. Study the books. Audiobooks or presentations are effective, too. Make your car a university on wheels by listening to them every time you are in your car.

Go to seminars and training sessions. Make the investment in you. You not only need the what, but you need the who. Assistance from experts is vital. Why would you try to do it alone when you can enroll the experts and eagles who have the experience and can help you achieve your goals? It is just a matter of asking and then learning and taking action. This is where you seek and then fly with the eagles. This is the law of return where you give and then it will all come back. Part of the give is to tap into the eagles and benefit from their knowledge through complimenting them and listening to their wisdom and then acting on their advice.

Knowledge is power. True eagles will always help. That's why they are eagles. They know that giving is the most powerful part of being an eagle.

## 9. Make a plan

What is your plan for action? What does it look like/ What are the timelines?

How have you prioritized them? Do you have a list in each of the areas out-lined above in step five? Plan and think on paper so your plan becomes engraved in your mind. Review and rewrite it over and over. It is an ever-evolving process. If you fail to plan, you're planning to fail.

## 10. Persist!

Resolve to never give up. Discipline is the bridge between your thought process-es and accomplishments. Discipline is a key ingredient that is the foundation for determination and persistence. Self-discipline is persistence in action. One undisciplined day at a time can add up to a year before you know it. The best plan on earth will not work unless you enact it through determination and per-sistence.

> *"The master in the art of living makes little distinction between his work and his play, his labor and his leisure, his mind and his body, his information and his recreation, his love and his religion. He hardly knows which is which. He simply pursues his vision of excellence at what he does, leaving others to decide whether he is working or playing. To him, he's always doing both."*
> *– Zen Buddhist saying*

# REPORT CARD TIME!

People who get the best grades know the answers to four very important questions.

Children always ask, "Why?" It's a good question. This is the first question.

Adults ask this question, too. You may be wondering, as you've been reading this book, *why* plan the next day the night before, *why* make ten calls before noon every day, *why* get up at 6 every day, *why* exercise, *why* give your time and money to others or charities, *why* …

Jim Rohn says the best answer to why is, "Why not?" Why not do all of the above? They all make sense. This is the second question to ponder.

The third question is, "Why not me?" Why aren't you eating at a café in Paris, staring at Michelangelo's masterpiece on the ceiling of the Sistine Chapel in Rome, walking along a beach on the French Riviera, sailing the Caribbean for two weeks with no cares in the world, standing at the top of the Grand Canyon in Arizona watching the sun set?

To paraphrase a statement by Jim Rohn, let's start to look at the future with anticipation, not apprehension.

There are so many people out there who have done so much with so little.

The final question to ponder is, "Why not now?" What is holding you back? Take action and do it now!

## Getting Straight A's

Oprah is a great example of a person who gets Straight A's. Her life story shows how attitude, aptitude, and action are a part of her everyday routine. She grew up in a tough environment and was constantly faced with adversity. Through sheer determination, persistence, and resolve, she not only survived but thrived.

She is now one of the most powerful people on the planet. So let's fill out her report card.

## Attitude  **A+**

This student is confident, secure, motivated, engaged, positive. She has great body language and leaves a wonderful impression. She is always in harmony with whatever situation comes her way. Her genuine enthusiasm for life is contagious. She makes every one in the class better just by experiencing her magic through her presence and attitude. A real winner!

## Aptitude  **A+**

This student has book smarts and influences hundreds of thousands of people to read. She has street smarts, too, and shows others how to get past their problems in order to achieve their promise. She is incredibly intelligent and wise with experience. A powerful combination.

## Action  **A+**

This student reaches out to everybody, regardless of background, race, or circumstances – from the poor to the rich and famous. Above all, she is a giver. She has spent her whole life giving. She not only has climbed the steep ladder to fame and fortune, but she also has helped others up along the way. She is not afraid to put herself out there for all to see. She is real. Her honesty shines through in everything she does. She has found something she loves to do and therefore it is not work, but pleasure and joy. This comes through in every show she does or every event she attends. Oprah has grace, eloquence, and confidence, not arrogance.

And here's the really great thing: there's nothing holding any of us back from becoming like this student, teacher, and mentor in our own way in our own situation. We can all get Straight A's!

# CHERISH THE MOMENTS

*"Living in the moment brings you a sense of reverence*
*for all of life's blessings."*
*– Oprah*

Thank you for reading *Tapping the Iceberg* to get an understanding of the Straight-A's philosophy of life. I would like to leave you with these closing thoughts as a way of celebrating with you the strides you have made by reading this book.

Certain moments shape us, define us, make us, break us, and control us. We have wonderful moments and moments we would like to forget. Moments are brief. They come and go in the blink of an eye.

Cherish the moments. Relive the moments. Savor the moments. Share the moments.

*"Life is not measured by the number of breaths we take,*
*but by the moments that take our breath away."*
*– Hilary Cooper*

Here's to moments and squeezing all we can out of every single one of them.

I appreciate the opportunity you have given me to share my ideas, concepts, and Straight-A's philosophy with you. My goal is to Touch, Inspire, and Move you to unleash your possibilities.

Tap into your attitude and aptitude. And take action to live a life full of happiness and success.